Let's START
WITH JESUS

Also by Dennis Kinlaw

This Day with the Master

DENNIS F.
KINLAW

Let's **START**
WITH JESUS

A NEW WAY OF DOING THEOLOGY

ZONDERVAN™

GRAND RAPIDS, MICHIGAN 49530 USA

ZONDERVAN™

Let's Start with Jesus
Copyright © 2005 by The Francis Asbury Society

Requests for information should be addressed to:

Zondervan, *Grand Rapids, Michigan 49530*

The Francis Asbury Society, P.O. Box 7, Wilmore, KY 40390–0007
www.francisasburysociety.com

Library of Congress Cataloging-in-Publication Data

Kinlaw, Dennis F., 1922–
     Let's start wtih Jesus : a new way of doing theology / Dennis F. Kinlaw.
         p. cm.
     Includes bibliographical references and index.
     ISBN: 978-0-310-26261-9
     1. Theology.   2. Jesus Christ—Person and offices.   I. Title.
BT77.K425 2005
230—dc22

2005008718

Interior design by Michelle Espinoza

To George Luce—
friend, mentor, great heart,
colleague in common cause

CONTENTS

CONTENTS

ACKNOWLEDGMENTS

For the person who believes in the triune nature of God, it is not difficult to understand that persons never come alone. They are always parts of webs of relationships that determine their character and their very being. If this is true of persons, it is usually true of their works, and it is certainly true of this one.

Any profitable insights found here result from meditations that have come out of the experiences of life and out of relationships with certain special persons over a third or more of a century. To trace them all here would be impossible. Certain ones, however, demand mention.

I have been privileged to be a part of a team of scholars and Christian leaders over these last seven years that has committed itself to try to find a more biblical way to approach systematic theology. The breadth of the group has been enriching to say the least. It has included professionals from the disciplines of philosophy, New Testament, Old Testament, systematic theology, historical theology, biblical theology, Christian education, and patristics. The group has included the ordained and unordained, clergy and laity, persons of both genders, and ones with experience in the pastorate, in evangelism, in teaching, and in missions.

The privilege of being a part of the dialogue–hearing and being heard and critiqued by those in common cause–has been a privilege beyond price. So to all of these people I must express my profound indebtedness. If there is any depth or relevance here, it is due in great measure to the profound understanding, Christian commitment, creativity, and passion for the propagation of the eternal gospel found in these colleagues. The present work is just a beginning, I am sure, of future and richer volumes that will come from this fellowship.

My tribute to Cricket Albertson, Paul Blair, Steve Blakemore, Chris Bounds, Harold Burgess, Gareth Cockerill, Allan Coppedge, Mary Fisher, Charlie Fiskeaux, Albert Luce, Burt Luce, Joe Luce, Tom McCall, John Oswalt, Mark Royster, Ron Smith, William Ury, and Paul Vincent.

PREFACE

One of the surprises in life for me has been that on certain occasions a single sentence from someone I respected has opened up a completely new world of conceptual possibilities. That happened for me one day in a class at Princeton Theological Seminary. The noted Pascalian scholar Emile Cailliet taught the course. It was titled "The Christian Pattern of Life." His syllabus listed three lectures under the heading "The Reformed Tradition of Holiness." In these lectures Dr. Cailliet presented his assessment of the development of the church's understanding of the doctrine of personal holiness through the centuries. When he came to the period of the Reformation, Dr. Cailliet made a simple statement that has affected my thinking ever since: "You can learn only one lesson at a time."

He explained that the battle that had to be won in the Reformation was that our salvation is by grace through faith alone, not by human works. He affirmed that the Reformers had left us deeply in their debt by defining for us more clearly than ever before the doctrine of justification by faith. Then he said, "But we do not turn to the Reformers for the classical development of the doctrine of personal holiness. That was not their battle." He then suggested that we would need to wait for the Evangelical Awakening in England in the eighteenth century for that. With those simple sentences, it dawned on me that progress is possible in our understanding of dogma and that one does not have to forfeit belief in the infallibility of the biblical revelation to believe that.

Somehow in my mind I had decided that the Christian faith had been delivered in the Hebrew Scriptures and in the New Testament in finished form, and it was simply our duty to repeat what had been revealed there. In other words, I felt that the orthodox Christian faith had been delivered to us in finalized form and that the business of the church was simply to declaim the Word given rather than to explore and share the profound implications of the revelation in the biblical text. Now I was confronted with the thought that there was more to be seen in Scripture than I had yet seen. My problem was not to seek something beyond the biblical text. It was to open myself as fully as possible to all that is buried within it. Slowly I began to realize how partially I understood the mystery of the gospel that has been given to us in Scripture and in Christ.

As I thought about this, I remembered the long struggle the church had to go through to understand and be able to proclaim simple truths, such as how Jesus of Nazareth could be both the son of Mary and at the same time the eternal Son of God. That naturally forced me to think of the three-centuries-long struggle the church fought in its effort to understand the biblical teachings on the relationship of the Father, the Son, and the Spirit to one another. The doctrine of the triune nature of God was the result, a doctrine without which our understanding of God, of ourselves as persons, of sin, and of redemption would be woefully inadequate.

That simple statement that individuals can learn only one lesson at a time has haunted me across the decades. Furthermore, it has changed my approach to Scripture and caused me to read it in a new way. Perhaps, I thought, it is true that we sit on the shoulders of those who have gone before us. If our perspective is larger than theirs, it is because of the work they did before us. That means that our relationship to them is one of great debt. It means that we dare not forfeit what they have seen lest we find ourselves in a "sea of legs" and have to start over. But it also means that perhaps we should in divine mercy, through the Spirit, be able to see farther, to see some things more clearly than they were able to see.

Slowly I began to realize that the juridical metaphor that was so liberating in the Reformation is biblical enough but that it is not the only metaphor that the Scriptures use to explain the heart of what Christ died to do for us. As I have lived with the biblical text across the years in pastoral preparation for preaching, seminary teaching, and in personal devotional research, the conviction has deepened within me that two other metaphors, the familial and the nuptial, permeate the whole of Scripture just as the forensic metaphor does. I realized that the juridical metaphor speaks of a role that God plays in relation to his creatures while the familial metaphor reveals to us, not just a role God plays, but insight into the very being of God. And the spousal nature of Christ's relationship to the church is the key to the purpose of human history (Mark 2:18–20 et al).

All of this, plus the needs of my own spirit, brought into focus the fact that through grace the cry of the human heart is for a personal knowledge of God more intimate than that which the judicial one pictures for us. I began also to realize that the picture of God himself that comes through these additional metaphors is far richer than that commonly assumed by most believers. I began also to realize that the message of the cross was taking on fuller, broader, and richer implications for me. It became clear that salvation is a gift of the Father through the Son and by the Spirit to bring me, not just to forgiveness and reconciliation with God, but into participation in the very communion that the three persons of the triune Godhead know between themselves. I began to feel that the key to understanding all of this was to start, not with the question of whether God exists and what can be known about him, but rather with Jesus himself who has assured us that he is the ultimate revelation of God. Jesus' word to Thomas became a word for me: "No one comes to the Father except through me. If you really knew me, you would know my Father as well. From now on, you do know him and have seen him" (John 14:6–7). If we get him, we get God; if we miss him, we miss God.

This exploration has been the most intellectually satisfying and the most spiritually challenging experience I have known. It has united theological exploration and worship into one. How exciting it is to find one's understanding of the nature of God producing a greater sense of adoration and praise, one's understanding of human sinfulness deepening one's humility and passion to be holy as Christ is holy, and one's understanding of God's purposes in the cross opening up dimensions of grace for personal communion with him and for life with others that make every day a joyous adventure.

The personal result for me of such thinking has been a journey of remarkable joy. It is that joy that lies behind the writing of this manuscript. I would like to think that in God's grace the thoughts in the pages that follow might prove to be at least in some small measure the blessing they have been to me.

One

A NEW CONCEPT OF GOD

A young chaplain at one of the colleges of Oxford University made it his practice every year to interview each new student in his college. He wanted to get to know each one and to explain something of the religious program in that college. On occasion, after the chaplain had made his case for the program, a freshman would explain a bit awkwardly that he did not believe in God and probably would not be active in the chaplain's program. The chaplain would then reply, "How interesting! And in which god do you not believe?" The student then would try to explain his atheism. The chaplain would smile and comment on the fact that he and the student had a great deal in common, for he did not believe in the existence of that god either.

Scholars have called *Homo sapiens* the religious creature. Wherever we find human beings, we find religious acts and religious language. God talk and human beings seem to go together. When a person speaks of *God* or of *gods*, what does he or she really mean? The common occurrence of the divine word in human language would seem to suggest that there is universal agreement as to its definition. However, the reality is quite the contrary.

Most of the gods that so-called unbelievers reject have never had any objective reality and are simply the goblin constructions of their own minds. The concept in their heads and the reality behind all things may have little relation to each other. The god before whom the sincere believer bows likewise may be a caricature that does little justice to the reality one believes oneself to be worshiping. The consequences for the believer whose mental understanding of God is skewed may not be as serious as would be the atheism of the person who denies God's very existence, but it is still damaging. Error for the believer, as well as for the unbeliever, always carries its unfortunate consequences.

William Temple, former Archbishop of Canterbury, insisted that if our concept of God is wrong, the more religious we get the more dangerous we are to ourselves and others. Our concept of God must be a true representation of the One Who Is, the God with whom all of us ultimately will have to deal. In fact, nothing is more important for anyone or for any society.

TWO KINDS OF GOD: POLY/PANTHEISTIC AND MONOTHEISTIC

But how can we know what God is really like? Yehezkel Kaufmann is helpful here.[1] In his signal work on the religion of Israel, he insists that all of the religions of the world can be put into two categories.

The first category includes all of those that are basically naturalistic and express themselves either in pantheism or polytheism. These religions see all things as an unbroken whole and the divine as part of that whole, or else they see the divine as a name for that whole in which we all participate. Some of these religions speak of the divine as that which permeates the whole and in which we all participate. This is pantheism as seen in Hinduism and contemporary New Age thought.

The other group in this category sees nature as containing the divine. The divine manifests itself in multiple forces, each of which has its own particular individuality and should be worshiped for itself. Thus, the Greeks could speak of *Ouranos* (the heavens), *Gaia* (the earth), *Oceanos* (the oceans), and *Chronos* (time) just as the Romans considered *Sol* (the sun) and *Luna* (the moon) primordial divine beings. The cultures of the ancient Mediterranean world had the same basic pantheon but used different names. Thus, the Greeks would speak of Aphrodite and the Romans of Venus, but both were speaking of the same factor in human life. We draw our word *aphrodisiac* from the name of Aphrodite. In speaking about Aphrodite and Venus, the Greeks and the Romans were referring to the erotic force that attracts the male to the female and the female to the male. Such natural forces were ascribed personhood and were worshiped as individual gods. We have known this polytheism classically in the religions of the ancient Near East and the Mediterranean world of Greece, Rome, and Egypt. Some version of it is found among most of the so-called primitive peoples of the earth. Today it is emerging in our postmodern world as New Age thought and practice.

Kaufmann's second group, the monotheistic religions, contains three distinct expressions, each of which is rooted not in nature (as are polytheism and pantheism) but in history. They are Judaism, Islam, and Christianity. One immediately recognizes that these are the three historic religions related to Israel and the Hebrew-Christian Bible. All three go back to Abraham and to his world for their roots. These three religions see nature not as divine but rather as a created expression of a supreme God who transcends that nature.[2] God is not a part of nature and must not be confused with anything within it. For these three religions, to mix nature and the divine is to be guilty of idolatry, the worship of that which has no existence in and of itself but is the product of one beyond itself, from which it comes and on which its very existence depends. In other words, these monotheistic religions all make an ontological distinction between the Creator and the creation.

The accuracy of Kaufmann's analysis is beyond debate.[3] This means that we are indebted to him for simplifying our problem, especially if we feel the need for a God who can actually make a significant difference in the human estate, a God who can help us. Polytheism and pantheism ultimately have no answer to the problem of evil because both see evil as part of the divine world and of the human world. For them what we speak of as "evil" and "divine" are not separable, for the evil of the world is included in the divine. There is nothing but "us." There is no "beyond" that is ontologically and morally different from us on which we can call or to which we can look for help. Therefore, history, like nature, is seen as repetitive, and the future cannot be essentially different from the past since there is no transcendent, transhistorical personal reality that makes a difference. On the other hand, the concepts of the possibility of a new world, a new society, and a different kind of human person have come into our culture from the Hebrew-Christian Scriptures because of the nature of the biblical God.

Kaufmann has helped us take the first step, but the second is equally important. There is one transcendent God, but what is that God's nature? A close reading of the literature of the three monotheistic religions will show radical differences among these three religious expressions and nowhere more than in their representations of the divine.

CHRISTIANITY: MONOTHEISM WITH A DIFFERENCE

There is no question that Judaism, Islam, and Christianity are monotheistic. The great basic truth behind Judaism is found in the Shema of Deuteronomy: "Hear, O Israel: The LORD our God, the LORD is one" (6:4). Old Testament texts made it clear that to be a Hebrew was to believe in one God, the God of Abraham, the God who brought Israel out of Egypt and who spoke to Moses on Sinai. The Hebrew prophets like Isaiah gloried in this: "I am the LORD, and there is no other; apart from me there is no God" (Isa. 45:5). Repetitively, Isaiah thunders this note (43:10; 44:8; 45:6, 14, 18, 21; et al.).

Subsequent Judaism has been unflinching on this. Maimonides, perhaps Judaism's greatest philosopher and jurist, set the pattern. Note his comments about circumcision, the symbolic rite that is the sign of the Abrahamic covenant:

> According to me circumcision has another very important meaning, namely that all people professing this opinion–that is, those who believe in the *unity of God*–should have a bodily sign uniting them so that one who does not belong to them should not be able to claim that he was one of them, while being a stranger.... *Circumcision* is a covenant made by *Abraham our Father* with a view to the belief in the *unity of God.* Thus everyone who is circumcised joins *Abraham's covenant.*[4]

Islam is equally clear in its affirmation that Allah is God and that he alone is God. The sin above all sins for the Qur'an is to affirm that there might be other gods than Allah. That theme begins early in the Qur'an and is everywhere the central assumption and affirmation.

Your God is one God; there is no God but He! He is the Beneficent, the Merciful.... Yet there are some men who take for
themselves objects of worship besides Allah, whom they love
as they should love Allah.... And O that the wrongdoers had
seen, when they see the chastisement, that power is wholly
Allah's, and that Allah is severe in chastising!... Thus will Allah
show them their deeds to be intense regret to them, and they
will not escape from the Fire. (2.163, 165, 167)

The Qur'an is particularly emphatic that Allah has no son (2116,
1935, 19:90–93, 112:3). He reigns alone.

Christianity joins with Judaism and Islam in their affirmation of the
oneness of God. Jesus firmly maintains that he and Moses stand in the
same tradition and worship the same God (John 5:45–46). God is one,
and he is to be loved with a single and exclusive devotion (Mark 12:29–
30). Paul, as a good Jew, trumpets his monotheism: "We know that an
idol is nothing at all in the world and that there is no God but one. For
even if there are so-called gods, whether in heaven or on earth ... yet
for us there is but one God, the Father, from whom all things came and
for whom we live" (1 Cor. 8:4–6). For the Christian, just as for the good
Jew and the devout Muslim, there is one God, and he alone is God.

But there is a difference. When Christians say that God is one, the
oneness of which we speak is not the same as the oneness of which
Jews and Muslims speak. It is not the unicity of a divine monad, of a
single divine being who is simple in nature. Christians believe that
within this oneness are personal differentiations. Note the passage we
just cited from Paul. He affirms the oneness of God but immediately
adds: "For us there is but one God, the Father, from whom all things
came and for whom we live; and there is but one Lord, Jesus Christ,
through whom all things came and through whom we live" (1 Cor. 8:6).
That addendum carries with it radical implications.

THE DIFFERENCE: JESUS

The world's problem with Christianity is Jesus. He is the "stone
that causes men to stumble" (1 Peter 2:8; cf. Rom. 9:32–33) that separates the monotheism of Christianity from that of Israel and Islam. And

the separation is absolute. This affects every aspect of Christian doctrine and gives distinction to its understanding of God, humanity, sin, salvation, and the *eschaton*.

The heart of the problem is Jesus' own understanding of who he is and of his relationship to God. The important data on this question are found in all of the New Testament gospels and epistles but are seen most clearly in the Gospel of John, especially in the unique passages where Jesus discusses his own relationship with God. The relationship he describes is very intimate. We see this particularly when he uses the word *Father*.

Although Jesus uses the term *Father* for God often in the other gospels, in John it occurs twice as many times as in Matthew, three times as often as in Luke, and six times as often as in Mark. He uses it so often in John that it is quite clear that the main character in the book, as in Jesus' life, is not himself but the Father. Christ and the Gospel of John point beyond themselves. They see Jesus as the "sent one" who has come from the Father to do the work of the Father. The language and syntax, the very grammar of the Gospel of John, show the centrality of this concept. John makes it clear that there was a unique intimacy between Jesus and the Father, one unlike that of God's relation to a prophet or even to Moses, who conversed with God face-to-face.

The fifth chapter of John presents this clearly. Jesus is in Jerusalem and sees a man lying at the pool of Bethesda. The man has been an invalid for thirty-eight years, apparently unable to walk. Jesus asks him if he wants to be well. When the man affirms that he does, Jesus tells him to get up, take up his mat, and walk. The man does as Jesus commands. It is the Sabbath, and the law of Moses forbids one to bear a burden on the Sabbath. Jesus' act shocks those in the temple courts. When the temple leaders learn that Jesus had ordered the sick man to take up his mat and carry it, they turn on him. They condemn him for a major violation of the Law. Jesus' response is cryptic. He informs them that his Father works on the Sabbath, and he is simply following his example.

The Jews accepted the fact that God worked on the Sabbath. How else could one explain the origin of rain or the birth of a baby when it came on the seventh day? These natural processes were seen as acts of a merciful and gracious God who cared about his people. So, Jesus asks, why should the Jews be shocked when he who is God's Son performs an act of mercy on the Sabbath? Should not a son act like his father?

The reasoning behind such an answer was not lost on these priests and temple leaders. Immediately they insisted that he was more than just a lawbreaker. He was putting himself on the same level with God, making himself equal with God. This, of course, was blasphemy to the good monotheistic Jew. Not surprisingly, the temple leadership immediately charged Jesus with that capital offense.

This accusation evoked from Jesus one of the most extended speeches in the Gospels on his relationship to Israel's God. He informed them that he was their God's Son and as such did nothing "by himself" (John 5:19). He was doing only what he saw his Father doing. The Father, Jesus insisted, shared with him all that he, the eternal God, did. He further explained that his Father, who is the source of life, shares his life with the Son. The Son does not have life in himself but draws it perpetually from the Father. The Father has all power, even the power to raise the dead, and has given that power to him, to Jesus the Son. In fact, the Father–the God of Israel, who is the Judge of all the earth–has given all judgment to him, Jesus the Son (v. 27).

The works that he was doing, like that of healing the sick man, evidenced that he was sent by the Father. This meant that they should be able to recognize him for who he was. John the Baptist had identified Jesus as the one for whom Israel looked (John 5:33, 36), and Moses himself, the greatest of all men, with the other prophets, had foretold his coming (vv. 46–47). This meant that Jesus should be honored just as the Father was honored because he is the Father's Son. Their failure to recognize him and to come to him meant, Jesus insisted, that they would miss the very life that he had graciously come to offer (vv. 39–40).

This speech, given after he had healed the man who had been lying sick for thirty-eight years, changed Jesus' relationship to the temple and to official Jerusalem. From that moment they determined to kill Jesus because he was assuming equality with God and thus was a blasphemer.

A subsequent miracle intensified the hostility of the temple officials to Jesus and underscored for them the necessity of his death. The account is found in John 9–10. It is the story of Jesus giving sight to the man born blind. Once again Jesus heals on the Sabbath, and immediately the case is brought to the attention of the temple leadership. John follows this story with Jesus' speech in which he calls himself the Good Shepherd who lays down his life for his sheep (10:11). He speaks in such an intimate way about God, his Father, that leaders challenge him. When he tells them that he and the Father are one, they pick up rocks to stone him because they realize he is claiming to be divine. Their attempt to kill Jesus fails as he slips through their hands. The temple officials now are convinced that he not only claims equality with God but that he claims a certain identity with him. Jesus must be destroyed.

Succeeding chapters in John give us other statements from the lips of Jesus that confirm the judgment of the Jewish leadership as to Jesus' self-understanding. The capstone of Jesus' claims comes in privacy on Thursday night of Holy Week in the upper room dialogue. Here he speaks not with the temple leaders but with his disciples, as later he will speak in their presence to his Father in the High Priestly Prayer in John 17. In these discourses, he insists that he and the Father are one. Indeed, they are so much one that anyone who has seen him has actually seen the Father, and in knowing him the disciples have actually known the Father (14:7, 9). The two, the Father and the Son, come together. Jesus makes it clear that his oneness with the Father is such that to reject him is to reject the Father and that to receive him is to receive the Father (13:20).

In recording these statements, John underlines and explicates Jesus' understanding of who he is. This understanding is implicit in all four gospels (cf. Matt. 10:40; 11:27; Mark 12:1–12; Luke 10:22) but is given in much richer detail and sharper focus in John.

Because of these speeches of Jesus, John concludes for himself that no one has ever seen the eternal God, but that Jesus, God's only Son, who has come from "the bosom of the Father," has actually made him known to us, has "exegeted" him to us (John 1:18 KJV; cf. Matt. 11:27). He sees Jesus as the Word of God, a Word who in the very beginning was with God, was actually divine himself, and brought all things into existence.

One does not have to be very familiar with Jewish literature to know that the opening verses of John's gospel, as they speak of the Word of God, are a paraphrasing of the beginning verses of the Genesis creation account. In John, however, something that is only implicit in Genesis, becomes explicit. In Genesis we learn that God created the world by speaking it into existence. The key phrase in Genesis 1 is "and God said." It is significant that the Hebrew word used for God (*Elohim*) is plural while the verb for "said" (*wayyo'mer*) is singular. In the beginning there was one God, but in that oneness there was a richness that a singular noun had difficulty conveying. With God was his Word, and the Word had its own distinctness. Thus, John could amplify the Genesis account and tell us that creation was the work of the Word of God.

That Word, we learn in the Gospels, is the eternal Son of the Father and has enough distinctness from the Father that he can become incarnate in a human virgin's fetus. God's Son, now incarnate in human flesh, is so identified with mortals that he will find himself in a garden praying to the Father for the grace to finish the work the Father has sent him to do. Yes, the Gospels tell us that God is one, but it is a different oneness than that which Jew or Muslim can affirm.

What the Gospels affirm about Jesus concerning his relationship to the Father is further developed in the rest of the New Testament. In Colossians 1:15 Paul says that Jesus is the very "image of the invisible God." Thus, Paul assents to John's witness that anyone who has seen Jesus has seen God. Like John, Paul insists that all things were created by him and for him and that all things are held together by him. In fact, in Jesus all the fullness of the Godhead dwells. The writer of Hebrews, in the introduction to his letter (1:1–4), develops this theme further by saying that Jesus is "the radiance of God's glory and the exact representation of his being," that he sustains all things "by his powerful word." The rest of the New Testament echoes and amplifies this thought.

The book of Revelation completes the picture. Jesus, the Lamb of God, is shown in 5:6 standing in the midst of the very throne of God. In the final scene (22:1–5), the throne of God, the seat of all divine power and authority, is identified as the throne both of God and of the Lamb, where the Lamb is being worshiped with the Father. Thus, in the *eschaton* the Jesus of the Gospels is receiving attributions reserved for deity. Obviously, the God pictured here is radically different from the God whom the temple leadership in Jesus' day conceived of and worshiped. This God is also very different from the Allah whom good Muslims have worshiped across the centuries. Jesus said that God is one, as Moses insisted, but in the oneness there is a differentiation that enables Jesus himself to be distinct from the Father and yet part of the divine oneness.

JESUS REVEALS THE NATURE OF GOD
God Is Familial

The character of that differentiation between Jesus and the Father is significant. Their unity is conceived in *familial* terms. Jesus insisted that his relationship to God is not servant but son, the only begotten Son of the Father. John's gospel most fully develops the theme, even though it is present elsewhere.

In the Old Testament the God of Israel is called "Father." The concept is introduced in Exodus when God tells Moses to instruct Pharaoh to let God's "son," Israel, go. So God describes his relationship to his own people as familial. Significantly, God speaks of Israel as his "firstborn" (Ex. 4:22). Implicit in the text is the indication that God intends to have more children. Israel is simply his first. This is one of the early missionary texts of the Bible.

When David is selected to be king of Israel, God says about him, "I will be his father, and he will be my son" (2 Sam. 7:14). With this as background, Israel understood the passage in Psalm 2:7 as a reference to David; there the psalmist quotes God as saying, "You are my Son; today I have become your Father." So now God and the king, as well as God and Israel, are seen as enjoying a familial relationship. The psalmist picks up this theme in Psalm 89:26–28. He describes how God has found David, chosen him from among the chosen people, and anointed him to be his vice-regent in Israel. He says of David:

> He will call out to me, "You are my Father,
>   my God, the Rock my Savior."

> *I will also appoint him my firstborn,*
>   *the most exalted of the kings of the earth.*
> *I will maintain my love to him forever,*
>   *and my covenant with him will never fail.*

Clearly, the relationship that Yahweh sees here is a familial one.

Subsequent Old Testament writers pick up this idea. Hosea can thus quote God as saying concerning Israel, "Out of Egypt I called my son" (Hos. 11:1). Jeremiah can quote God saying to Israel, "Have you not just called to me: 'My father, my friend from my youth, will you always be angry?'" (Jer. 3:4–5). Other prophets assume this as an acceptable metaphor.

Implicit within the larger Old Testament text, and occasionally becoming explicit, is the notion that Yahweh clearly sees himself in a paternal relationship with specific individuals other than just the king. We see this particularly in his relationship with the needy, orphans, widows, and foreigners. Note the following from Psalm 68:4–6:

> *Sing to God, sing praise to his name,*
>   *extol him who rides on the clouds–*
> *his name is the LORD–*
>   *and rejoice before him.*
> *A father to the fatherless, a defender of widows,*
>   *is God in his holy dwelling.*
> *God sets the lonely in families,*
>   *he leads forth the prisoners with singing;*
>   *but the rebellious live in a sun-scorched land.*

We have here an implicit affirmation that Yahweh is the sovereign Judge who will fight for justice for the alien, be father to the orphan, and protect the woman who has lost her husband. The paternal character of Yahweh's relationship to humans permeates the Old Testament. He is like a father to his own.

Normally the fatherhood of God in these passages is interpreted as analogical. This is particularly true when we begin our study of God with his being rather than with his Son. The relationships between God and

Israel and between God and David are seen as *like* that between a father and a son. Yet when Jesus speaks of his relationship to God, he complicates matters. When he speaks of his relationship to God, he employs different terms. His point of reference is not the human family, but the nature of God himself, the God who Jesus says was a Father before there was a human family. He is talking metaphysics, not metaphor–ontology, not analogy. His relationship with God is not like that of a human son with a human father. The relationship between the Father and Son is the prototype (original) of which all human familial relations are ectypes (copies). The relationship of which he is speaking is the original to which all human familial relationships are analogical.

Jesus saw his filial relationship to God as one that preceded Bethlehem; in fact, it existed from before creation. For him it was eternal. God is his eternal Father, and he is God's eternal Son. The relationship is unique, unshared by anyone else. John's understanding prompted him to speak of Jesus as God's "only begotten" Son. The relationship of human believers to God reflects that of Jesus and the Father, but it is not the same. Jesus' relationship to his Father is the original after which all human filial relationships, both physical and spiritual, are patterned. Note the assumptions behind Paul's utterance to the Ephesians in 3:14–15: "For this reason I kneel before the Father, from whom his whole family in heaven and on earth derives its name."

For Jesus this filial relationship was the primary way he interpreted his relation to the eternal. The language of the Gospels, especially the syntax of the Greek text, gives dramatic witness to this. In the English translation we read, "And the Father who sent me has himself testified concerning me" (John 5:37). The literal translation of the Greek poignantly expresses it: "And the-sending-me-Father, that one has testified concerning me." The Father is primary in everything about Jesus. Jesus is the Son whom the Father has sent. This theme is not just a Johannine one, for it is found in the Synoptics (cf. Matt. 11:25–27; Mark 12:1–12; Luke 10:21–22). In the four gospels we find the term *Father* occurring no less than 170 times. Jesus is revealing a different and richer understanding of the nature of God. A new paradigm is being developed.

The remainder of the New Testament picks up this theme from Jesus' statements in the Gospels. The first thing Paul says about God in almost every letter is that God is Father. His most common greeting to the churches to which he writes is, "Grace to you and peace from God our Father and from the Lord Jesus Christ." First Peter begins with almost identical words. James speaks of the power of the tongue, reminding us that we use it to bless "our Lord and Father" and curse those made in his image (3:9). The writer of Hebrews in 1:1–5 tells us of the superiority of the new dispensation. In the former dispensation God spoke to us through prophets. Now God has spoken to us "by his Son," one who is the "exact representation of [God's] being," through whom all things were created and all things are sustained. God identifies Jesus as his Son, a relationship superior even to that of angels. Angels were created. The Son was begotten. In the little book of Jude, the author identifies those to whom he writes as those "who have been called, who are loved by God the Father and kept by Jesus Christ" (v. 1).

A significant change was taking place in New Testament times regarding the understanding of God. The creature normally thinks of God in relation to the creation. The questions of his existence and his relationship to the creation seem primary to us. Thus, systematic theologians since Augustine have begun their work with questions about the being of God. This places the emphasis, after we have decided we can believe that God exists, on the attributes of his being–such abstract qualities as infinity, eternity, omnipotence, omniscience, unchangeableness, and impassibility. Jesus clearly is leading us in a very different approach. When Jesus is sending out the Seventy-two, he says: "No one knows who the Son is except the Father, and no one knows who the Father is except the Son and those to whom the Son chooses to reveal him" (Luke 10:22).

Jesus has a unique role in the revelation of God. In John he refers to himself as "the door" (10:7 KJV). Jesus thinks of himself not only as the door into salvation but also into the knowledge of the one true God. Logically this means we should begin our theological studies with Jesus, who, as John said, "has made him known" (John 1:18).

Jesus insists that he is a window on the inner life of God himself, not on just how God relates to his world. Later the church fathers used two phrases to express this. They spoke of seeing God "from the outside" (*ab extra*) and "from the inside" (*ab intra*). We as creatures only can see him from the outside. Jesus' claim is that he knows and sees God from the inside. What he sees is familial, and the familial character is not an attribute of God but his actual ontological nature. If there is life in God, it is a shared life between Father and Son. This is further proof that we should begin our theological studies with Jesus.

Paul understood what Jesus was indicating. For Paul, Jesus was saying that the first word to be said about God is that he is Father. But Paul suggests in 1 Corinthians 15:24 that the last word that can be said about God also will be familial. Fatherhood is not a passing role that God plays in relationship to Jesus. Paul explains that Christ will ultimately reign, that every knee will bow and acknowledge him as Lord. Then Jesus will render up his kingdom to the Father from whence it came (1 Cor. 15:24). The original picture is of a family, not a court; and the ultimate context for the redeemed will be familial as well as legal. Terms like *King, Judge*, and *Sovereign* speak of what God does, of his relationship to the creation. *Father* speaks of who he is in himself eternally apart from the creation, and the kind of spiritual relationship he wants with all persons in his creation.

Thus, a different concept of God is emerging. The writer of Revelation picks up this theme when he speaks of the final scene in human history. The NRSV tells us that those who inherit the final kingdom will hear God say, "I will be their God and they will be my children" (Rev. 21:7). He is the eternal Father.

God Is Self-Giving Love

Basic to the New Testament understanding of God is this insistence that God is one, that there is differentiation in the oneness, and that the difference is familial. In Jesus' picture of the life of God as seen "from the inside"–God's life as Jesus sees and experiences it–we discover the key to comprehending God: *self-giving love*. Jesus affirms repeatedly that the Father loves the Son. In fact, this love is eternal; it was there before the foundation of the world. And it is self-giving love. The Father has life in himself and gives this life to his Son. In such love the Son knows that all that the Father has is his. Nothing is withheld. The Son's response is other-oriented, self-giving love–love that causes the Son not to delight in doing his own will but in doing the will of the Father. We should not be surprised, then, when we find the author of 1 John giving us a new definition for God: God *is* love (1 John 4:8, 16). Love is not just something God does, but it is what he actually is. Love is his inner life, the divine life, which the three persons of the blessed Trinity co-inherently share.

The monotheism of Islam and Judaism and that of Christianity are radically different in respect to God's love. Love is an interpersonal reality. It speaks of the possible relationship of one person to another. Thus, it is by definition other-oriented.[5] There must be two for love to exist, the lover and the one loved. One needs an *other* to love. Jesus indicates that in the inner being of the Godhead there is otherness and that the relationship is one of self-giving love. The obvious proofs of the love of God for us are in the incarnation and the cross, where Jesus sacrificed his life in love for us. But Jesus says that the Father loves him in the same way that he, Christ, loves us. The greatest possible expression of love, Jesus says, is to lay down one's life for another. The Father gives life to the Son, who returns that life to the Father. The Father asked the Son to come to earth, become a human being, and give his life so the world might be saved. The Son joyously did as his Father desired. With this new understanding of the nature of God comes a new concept of love as well–a love determined by the nature of the subject who loves rather than by the nature of the object loved.

A comparison of the biblical idea of love with the Platonic idea of love illustrates the uniqueness of the biblical perspective. Plato gives a revealing picture of Socrates in *The Symposium*. Socrates reports to his friends how a wise woman explained to him that love is not something the greatest of the gods can experience. She said that to love means to desire; and desire is an indication of need. We love another because the other meets a need in our own experience. We know that the great gods are perfect and have no needs. Therefore, how can the gods love? The assumption behind Plato's whole discussion is the conviction that the lover seeks in the beloved the fulfillment of the lover's own needs. Socrates could not conceive of love that was primarily concerned with what the lover could *do for* the loved rather than what the lover could *acquire from* the loved. To Socrates love is self-oriented and concerned with how the other can satisfy the needs of the lover.

The unique picture of love Jesus presents was the exact opposite of the picture that the wise men of his world understood. Jesus embodies the Old Testament revelation of God's *hesed*, or "steadfast love," seen in God's faithful love of Israel throughout the Old Testament. This love of God is a love relationship in which the lover loves not for what can be acquired, but for what can be given to meet the needs of the beloved. In fact, giving is the lover's greatest joy. The true fulfillment in Jesus' paradigm is in no way related to self-satisfaction unless a person comes to the place where the other's welfare is more important than his or her own. Jesus' paradigm is of one who loves to give whether the recipient responds or not. For Jesus love is the giving of oneself to and for the one loved. Greek has no word to express that thought because such a thought is not natural to human beings as we know human beings.[6]

The early Christian writers of the New Testament had to develop their own vocabulary to express their message. They had to inject language that reflected humanity's fallen state with new meaning. Thus, they took a noun (*agapé*) that hardly occurs in classical Greek, poured into it their own meaning, and adopted it to speak of the nature of the relationship that characterizes the inner life of God. The thought of a love that cares more for another than for itself was formed and nominally and verbally expressed. That understanding then came to predominate the meaning of the Greek verbal root (*agapao*) from which the noun was formed. The New Testament writers and the fathers of the early church then had the linguistic equipment necessary to describe this God who is seen in Jesus Christ, his essential nature, and his relation to us. Something new had entered fallen human thought. The prophet Isaiah had a foreglimpse of this new thought when he asked, "Who has believed our message?" (53:1). To the one who does not know Christ, the story of Christ is unbelievable. But in Christ and the cross such love has been seen, and with the church's new vocabulary the story can be told.

God Is Dialogical

The insistence that other-oriented relationships are at the very heart of the nature of God led to another insight about the inner life and character of God. There is communication between the persons of the Godhead. They are in a relationship of dialogue, which is reflected in the creation of the world. John develops this in his concept of the Word. The beginning of his gospel, as stated above, is a development of the understanding of the creation, found in Genesis 1.

John tells us that the Word was "in the beginning" and the Word "was God." When Genesis says, "In the beginning God created the heavens and the earth," the phrase "In the beginning" speaks of the period before anything existed but God. A close look at John 1 will confirm that the phrase "In the beginning" there has the same meaning. John is speaking of the "time" when there was nothing but God, and the Word was *with* God, and the Word *was* God. God, then, is a one, but he is not one alone. There is an otherness in the oneness, and that otherness can be described as the Word. This means that the inner life of God is *dialogical.* In the beginning there was God and his Word. So creation began with a conversation.

Brian Horne, thinking of the fact that the God of Scripture talks, reminds us that George Steiner has said, "God is capable of all speech-acts except that of monologue." Horne, on the basis of this statement, insists that God's capacity for dialogue makes possible "our acts of reply, of question and counter-question." But the original dialogue is not with us. That conversation takes place within the inner personal life of the Trinity. Horne, therefore, can say:

> This Hebraic notion of dialogue with the Creator–a kind of absolute freedom to answer back–is, however as far as the Christian is concerned, superseded by the notion of a dialogue which–if the term may be permitted–precedes the original act of creation: a conversation of the persons within God the Trinity. God speaking Himself in His Word and hearing Himself in

His Spirit: expressing Himself in His Son and receiving Himself in His Spirit. It is not by any other than a Trinitarian action that the world is brought into and sustained in being. The answer the creatures make is, like prayer, not so much reply to God–our dialogue with Him–but a participation in a dialogue which already exists–the eternal conversation of God Himself.[7]

A word is a means of interpersonal communication. Only persons, not animals or things, have words. Persons can speak, yet when they speak they must speak to another. Words indicate interrelatedness. So, in the beginning when there was nothing but God alone, there was communication. From what Jesus says about the inner life of God, apparently one person was speaking to another. This should not be too surprising since there are different persons in the Godhead and those persons are related by love. It is the nature of love to communicate. Ultimately love, if it can speak, cannot remain quiet.

So the God of Scripture is a speaking God. And when he speaks, the communication not only is love, but more. His speaking is creative. Genesis gives evidence of this. One can make a strong case for the fact that the key to Genesis lies in the simple phrase, "And God said." Note its occurrence not only in the creation story, but also throughout the book. Every significant development begins with that phrase. God speaks to someone, and circumstances are new. The prophets pick up this theme about God and glory in it. They find a major contrast between the God of Israel and all other gods of the world. Their God speaks; idols do not (note 1 Kings 18:26; Isa. 46:7; Jer. 10:5).

God Is Free

God in his inner life is one, and yet that oneness is a communion of other-oriented, self-giving love. This forces us to acknowledge another factor that enriches our vision. The inner life of God is characterized by *responsible freedom*. There is no external force beyond God in his oneness or beyond the persons within that oneness. Sovereignty characterizes the relationship of God to his creation, but that is not a factor in the inner life of God. Other-oriented love among equals reigns there, and love is possible only where freedom rules. The Father may play a different role than the Son, but the relationship is between persons who in essence are equals. The temple leadership understood this. After the healing on the Sabbath of the invalid at the pool of Bethesda, they accused Jesus of making himself equal to God. After Jesus bestowed sight on the man blind from birth (John 9), the officials insisted he was actually claiming to be God (10:33). Jesus did not deny their charge. He simply affirmed that he was doing his Father's business and doing it as a labor of self-sacrificial love.

There was no compulsion in this relationship between Father and Son. Jesus' relationship to the Father was characterized by love, not necessity, and responsible freedom in love. Authority had been given to him by the Father so he could do his Father's will, but he did it because he chose freely to do so. He would lay down his life for the world to please his Father, but by his own free choice. His sacrifice was not forced upon him. It would be a voluntary act, a sacrifice of double-edged love. He wanted to please his Father, and he loved the world. He *chose* to die; he was no martyr. His life was not taken from him; he gave it. This fact makes the cross a window through which we so clearly can see the nature of God. The Father and the Son are one in this act. We see God for who he really is. Jesus' life was one of free, loving obedience to his Father. His only autonomous decision, as John indicates, was to do the will of his Father, and that he did freely (John 10:18). The window of the incarnation and the cross gives us a picture of the inner being of God as a communion of free, other-oriented persons living in a dialogue of self-giving love. This God, Jesus insists, is the God of Israel who called himself holy and commanded us to be the same.

Understanding God as a Trinity of free persons gives us one of the most striking differences between the monotheism of Christianity and the other monotheistic religions. In Judaism and Islam God is a single being without rival or competitor; he reigns alone and unchallenged. The emphasis in these two religions is primarily upon God's single sovereign will: he needs to give account to no one. If God is capricious, his caprice is right because he alone is God. If he loves, it is something he does, one of his volitional acts. It is not who he is. If he is merciful, it is a decision he makes, not necessarily an expression of his eternal nature.

These beliefs create the ambience in which God and his worshipers live and move. In these monotheisms the emphasis is primarily on performance, on obedience to the sovereign will of the sovereign God. Salvation is a reward for one's obedience. On the other hand, in Christianity the will of God is also supreme, but his will is conditioned by the interrelatedness in love of the three persons that constitute the Godhead. The interpersonal context is crucial, providing an atmosphere of trust rather than mere external conformity, and providing salvation as a gift of grace rather than a reward for one's good works.

God Is Triune

Jesus made the difference between the monotheism of Christianity and that of Judaism and Islam even clearer by teaching that the inner life of God is *more than bipolar*—more than the Father and the Son. The divine Being is *triune.*

On the night before Jesus' crucifixion, the disciples finally realized that Jesus was about to leave them. They declared to him their deep distress. He had become their life, and they found it unthinkable that they could live without him. He had a word of comfort. He let them know that he was not leaving them alone. He was sending one to them to take his place, the Spirit of truth himself. He described this Spirit as "another Comforter" (John 14:16 KJV). What Jesus had been to them, the Spirit would be all that and more. He is "another" comforter, but he is enough like Jesus that he can take Jesus' place in the disciples' lives. In fact, he will be able to do for them things that Jesus as the incarnate Son could not do. Jesus indicates that in the coming of the Spirit, he himself will actually be coming too, but in a new way (vv. 18, 28). A primary role of the Spirit will be to give them a sense of communion with him as their risen Lord.

The language the New Testament uses when it speaks of the Spirit is significant. Two Greek words are commonly used in the New Testament to express otherness. The first is used of *another* of the *same* kind. The second is used of *another* of a *different* kind. Although this distinction may not be without exception, the differentiation is maintained consistently enough to indicate that the author of the text was saying that the Spirit was *"another of the same kind"* as Jesus. This Comforter will take the place of the physical presence of Christ; lead Jesus' followers into the deeper dimensions of truth that God has for them; convict of sin, righteousness, and judgment; continue the work that Christ had been doing in the world; and intensify their sense of his presence with them.

The early church fathers forged the doctrine of the triune Being of God. The emergence of the concept of the Spirit as a person in the God-head should not have been totally unexpected. They were familiar with all of the data in the Old Testament about the Spirit, which now began to make more sense. The role of the Spirit in the Old Testament is quite prominent. He has a relationship to the natural world and seems to be the key to its well-being. The Spirit is pictured as hovering in those moments of creation over the dark waters (Gen. 1:2). The psalmist speaks of how the Spirit renews the face of the earth and gives life to its creatures (104:30). Isaiah describes the Spirit as transforming the desert into a fertile field (32:15).

It is, however, in the lives of the Old Testament's most important characters that the Spirit's presence and work are seen most graphi-cally. Moses, Bezalel, Joshua, Othniel, Gideon, Jephthah, Samson, Saul, David, and the prophets all are described as having the presence of the Spirit in and upon their lives. From the Old Testament's point of view, the answer to every major national problem seemed to be the coming of one upon whom the Spirit rested. Little wonder that the Old Testa-ment makes the presence of the Spirit the supreme characteristic of the one for whom Israel waited–the Messiah, the Anointed One. The Spirit of the Lord was to rest upon him. What's more, the mark of the new age, which the Messiah would inaugurate, would be the outpouring of the Spirit upon all flesh, not just upon God's firstborn, Israel. His ministry was to be universal. John Oswalt is on target when he says: "In fact, we might go so far as to say that except for Isaiah 53 the connection between the Messiah and the giving of the Holy Spirit is considerably clearer in the Old Testament than is his atoning death and resurrection. This is not to suggest in any way that these emphases are not present in the Old Testament, but it is simply to say that sometimes modern Christian teaching makes primary what the Old Testament does not."[8]

Such thoughts were in the minds of the fathers as they wrestled with the words of Jesus about the Spirit.

Another factor also moved the early fathers deeply: the nature of the love Jesus demonstrated that flowed within the inner life between the Father and the Son. As the thinking of the early church developed and as they tried to grasp the glory of the inner life of the God whom Jesus had revealed to them, the actuality of the existence of the Spirit as a third person within the Godhead became more and more reasonable. Walter Kasper makes clear the process of thought in the early church that led to the development of the doctrine of the Trinity:

> Each of the three modes in which the one love of God subsists is conceivable only in relation to the other two. The Father as pure self-giving cannot exist without the Son who receives. But since the Son does not receive something but everything, he exists only in and through the giving and receiving. On the other hand, he would not have truly received the self-giving of the Father were he to keep it for himself and not give it back. He exists therefore insofar as he receives himself wholly from the Father and gives himself wholly back to the Father, or, as it is put in the farewell prayer of Jesus, glorifies the Father in his turn. As an existence that is wholly owed to another, the Son is therefore pure gratitude, eternal Eucharist, pure obedient response to the word and will of the Father. But this reciprocal love also presses beyond itself; it is pure giving only if it empties itself of, and gives away, even this two-in-oneness and, in pure gratuitousness, incorporates a third in whom love exists as pure receiving, a third who therefore exists only insofar as he receives his being from the mutual love between Father and Son. The three persons of the Trinity are thus pure relationality; they are relations in which the one nature of God exists in three distinct and non-interchangeable ways. They are subsistent relations.[9]

What Jesus started when he insisted that God was his Father and that he and the Father were one was a complete revolution in the human understanding of the divine and of humankind's relationship to it. Those who knew Christ and accepted his teachings could never think of God in the same way again. It would take centuries for the church to think through the implications of what they had learned in Jesus. An intellectual revolution had begun that was to be without equal in human history in understanding God, the world, and the human creature. The only thing analogous in the history of human thought is the revolution in the understanding of God that came to and through Moses in the Exodus and Sinai experiences. At that time, human persons were able to break out of Kauffman's first group of religions, the ones rooted in nature with no transcendent personal creator. The Genesis doctrine of *creatio ex nihilo* was at the heart of that revolution. The Old Testament gives us a special testimony to the development of the insights implicit in the revelation that came to Moses. Isaiah, building on Moses, gives us a rich picture of a God who is one and one alone, without rival or competitor, whose purposes for his creation are fully redemptive. Hear Yahweh as he speaks through his prophet.

> *I am the LORD, and there is no other;*
>   *apart from me there is no God.*
> *I will strengthen you,*
>   *though you have not acknowledged me,*
> *so that from the rising of the sun*
>   *to the place of its setting*
> *men may know that there is none besides me.*
> *I am the LORD, and there is no other.*
> *I form the light and create darkness,*
> *I bring prosperity and create disaster;*
> *I, the LORD, do all these things. (45:5–7)*

So Moses gave to the world a new understanding of a God beyond all gods, one God who created out of nothing all that exists. God is one, but that oneness is not that of unicity. Rather, it is marked by an inner interpersonal love among the persons of the Trinity. The diversity in the oneness is the second great intellectual revolution, and it took the church centuries to articulate clearly what Jesus had revealed.

God Is Holy

Because of the transcendence of Yahweh, it was inevitable that a sense of difference would develop in the Old Testament in the relationship between Israel and God. He was ontologically distinct from his creation, separated in his essence from all his creatures by a metaphysically uncrossable chasm. He alone can say of himself "I am." All others must say, "I am because of him." As theologians say, he alone has subsistence in himself. All the rest of us derive our existence from him and subsist because of him.

That difference is more than ontological. God's character as the ultimate absolute is different. It is moral and ethical. In fact, it is in his otherness that the differentiation between right and wrong, good and evil, true and false have their origin. The true, the good, and the righteous are not true and good and righteous because of their conformity to some standard set by Yahweh. He is the standard for and the actual source of all that is true and good and right. This otherness comes to be expressed in the Old Testament by the word Yahweh claims as his own, the word *holy*. In the Old Testament he comes to be called "the Holy One." If anything else possesses any holiness, it is because of its association with him. He says of himself, "I am the LORD, who makes you holy" (Lev. 22:32 et al.). And his command to his people is, "Be holy because I, the LORD your God, am holy" (Lev. 19:2). We should not be surprised to find when we come to the New Testament that those who are followers of Christ and who believe in the God of the Old Testament are called saints, "the holy ones."

The development of the concept of the holy is one of the striking etymological stories in the Bible. The first use of the word *holy* as it is applied to anyone is found in Genesis 38 where Tamar, the daughter-in-law of Judah, is identified in the original language as a "holy woman." In Canaan part of the "ministry" of temple priestesses was cult prostitution, so a priestess was called a "holy woman" and served as a prostitute. So the biblical text uses the term "holy woman" for Tamar because she was playing the role of the prostitute with Judah.

In Exodus the evolution of the biblical word *holy* begins to occur. The next use of the term is in Exodus 3 where God confronts Moses from the burning bush. God tells Moses to take off his shoes. The ground on which he is standing is holy because God, the Holy One, is present. After this, the Hebrew word for holy (*qadesh*) becomes Yahweh's particular property. He fills it with new meaning that speaks of his being and character.

God pours his own nature into the word at Mount Sinai when he seals his covenant with the people of Israel, whom he has redeemed from Egyptian bondage. He tells them they are to be a "kingdom of priests" and a "holy nation." Yahweh the Holy One wants them to be his own; he wants to dwell in their midst. The symbols of his presence are fire and the Decalogue—the Ten Commandments. The fire speaks of his otherness. The Decalogue gives the relationship moral content. Their relationship is to be one marked by awe, reverence, proper fear, gratitude, adoration, and worship. It is also to be characterized by right relationships not only with Yahweh, but also with all others.

In Hebrew the Ten Commandments are called simply the "Ten Words." The first four of these words concern the proper relationship of God's people to him, to his name, and to his gift of time. He is to be central in our lives, speech, and time. Devotion to God must permeate the totality of our existence. The fifth word speaks of our relationship to our parents. We are to *honor* our parents. Honor makes obedience natural for a child. The sixth through the ninth have to do with the sanctity of another's life, sexuality, property, and reputation. The tenth addresses our attitude toward the providence of God in our lives. We must not be discontented with God's provision for us.

Yahweh's concern is for righteousness in his people, defined simply as right relations with all in our personal world. The commands reflect the fact that Yahweh is the Holy One. To have his presence in our life, we must relish the same rightness in all personal relations that Yahweh does. As he is the ontological source from which all being comes, he is also the pure fount from which all that is holy and right flows. The philosophers speak of God's being and his acts as one, while our being and acts can be separated. Our unity has been shattered by sin, by the fall, but his has not. What he is and what he does are totally consonant. His acts can be taken as revelatory of who he is. The economic

trinity (who God has revealed himself to be in history) and the immanental Trinity (who God is in himself) are one. God is the same in his
essence as he is in the revelation of Jesus Christ—the final revelation of
God. So a basic tension exists between God as the Holy One and us in
our fragmentation.

This incompatibility between God and his creatures is shown
graphically in Isaiah's experience in the temple when he is confronted
with God on his throne (Isa. 6). In an individual experience that is
remarkably like the corporate experience of Israel at Sinai, the prophet
is smitten with the difference between himself and Yahweh. The over-
tones of power and deity encompass him, but it is not the attributes of
God that overwhelm him. Yahweh's overwhelming power and deity are
real enough, but the thing that undoes Isaiah is Yahweh's holiness.
Power is something Yahweh possesses, but holiness is who he is. Isaiah's
problem is his own unholiness, his own moral and ethical uncleanness.
But a living coal from the divine altar cleanses him, and he becomes fit
for the presence and service of Yahweh.

A key to grasping the entire biblical picture is the nature of the
third person of the Godhead, the Spirit. He is most commonly desig-
nated as the Holy Spirit. When Jesus was defining his individual distinctness and ministry, he spoke of his purpose. The Father is the one
who gives us the Son to save us, and the Son gives himself to reconcile
us to himself. Likewise, the Spirit comes to let us know our need of a
savior. He is the one who convinces us of our sin, our need for righteousness, and the threat of judgment if we do not find reconciliation
and redemption. He does this simply by being himself, the Holy Spirit.
He is the Spirit of God, the God who is the Holy One.

The moral uniqueness of Yahweh was as real as his ontological
uniqueness and almost more significant in understanding personhood.
Greek philosophers could speak of the "ultimacy of being" as a general
concept and include within that term the divine, but the Hebrews knew
from bitter experience that the being of Yahweh and the being of his
human creatures were two eternally and significantly different kinds
of reality. First, the creature does not share the divine nature of the Creator; the ontology is different. Second, the creature does not share the

moral character of his or her Maker. No human being is by nature holy. Human persons are made for holiness, but it is a derived characteristic for the human person, and the origin of any holiness that the creature ever knew or will ever know comes through intimate personal contact with the Holy One. In fact, it comes only as the creature shares in the very life of God. The source of all holiness is God alone.

JESUS REVEALS THE PURPOSES OF GOD: INTIMACY WITH HIS CREATURES

The Old Covenant: God among His People

The fact that the Holy One desires a personal, intimate relationship with his creatures inevitably creates tension. The purpose of creation was for God to have persons with whom he could fellowship in love. At the climax of the creation story, Yahweh comes down in the cool of the day and seeks his creatures. The God who is seen in the New Testament figure of Christ knocking at the door and of the Good Shepherd seeking his one lost sheep is the same God who made all things and seeks fellowship with his children. The creation was to find its fulfillment in a fellowship of trusting, self-giving love. The relationship of Yahweh and Abraham is described as friendship. The figure is that of friends walking together.

The book of Exodus clearly describes God's desire for a relationship of trusting, self-giving love with all of his people. The climax of Exodus is the construction of the tabernacle so that God can dwell in the midst of his people. What was to make Israel distinct among the nations was God's saving presence in their very midst. The lengthy detail in the book of Exodus on how the tabernacle was to be built is not there to bore us but to let us know that God wants to live in intimacy with his creatures. His name is Immanuel, God with us.

But God's creatures are not like him. He is holy by nature, and they, because of their sin, are not. He is righteous by definition, but they, because of the fall, are not. He is the source of all that is good, and they, because they have separated themselves from him, are not good. He is love and cares profoundly for his creatures, but they have centered themselves in themselves and are willing to use others for their own ends. God's love for the holy and the good makes him hostile to the destructiveness of all that is not holy and good. In fact, the Old Testament insists that such actually angers God and provokes the divine wrath. His very goodness means that he must destroy the evil. This puts a dangerous tension in the relationship between humans, with their sinful bent, and God, who is holy-love itself.

We see this concept in the architecture and ritual of the temple. The gradations of access to the temple interior and the system of sacrificial offerings point to the deadly seriousness of one's relationship to God. If it is right, it is the very source of life. If it is wrong, the promise for death–eternal death–is inherent within it. The innermost room of the temple was called the Holy of Holies because it was there that the Holy One dwelt between the cherubim. His throne had within it the tablets of the law Moses had received on the mountain. One could not have fellowship with God apart from the presence of that law. Not even the high priest, who alone entered the Holy of Holies to represent himself and his people, could enter without a bloody sacrificial offering given to provide covering for the priest's sin. There could be no fellowship with this God apart from a sacrifice of life. Yet this Holy One sought fellowship with those so different from him.

The very ambience of the temple spoke of God's otherness. Yet the atmosphere also was redolent with indications that Yahweh sought intimate communion with his people. In fact, God wanted his people to be like him. At the heart of the instructions about the tabernacle and its ways of worship was the command from Yahweh: "Be holy, for I am holy." But if the people were to be like him, they had to know what he was like. God did not interject this sense of tension to deter his people from having close and intimate fellowship with him. Rather, he did it to ensure that they did not miss his presence. It was to protect them from the trap of assuming a fellowship with God that, in reality, is merely a religious communion with oneself.

One of the prime evidences that God wanted Israel for himself in a very special and unique relationship is that he made known to them his name. It was given to Moses and was Israel's most precious possession. They became "the people of the name." When one knows another's name, one has a relationship with that person that others do not have. In fact, there is a sense in which to know a person's name is to have at least a measure of control over his or her attention. When Yahweh gave Israel his name, it meant "You can have my attention in a very special and personal way." However, there was a condition. It was not to be used carelessly. One of the Ten Commandments addresses this matter (Ex. 20:7). God's people were not to use it vainly. In fact, the Hebrews became so afraid of misusing it that they began to substitute the title *Lord* for his personal name.[10]

Although God had given his people his own name and desired communion with them, they decided to do things their way and put their trust, not in their Maker and Sustainer, but in themselves. Since God is the source of life and good, separation from him meant the advent of evil and death. Because God knew the destructive potential of humanity's rebellion, the unbelievably tragic consequences that would result, and the total perversion of his purposes for creation, God found himself angered by human sin.

The New Covenant: God Is One with His People

God's desire for intimacy with his creation became even more obvious with the appearance of Christ. The desire—expressed and implicit in the old covenant—is more fully evident in the incarnation. God does not simply want to dwell in the temple among his people. He takes on flesh so he can be one with us and gives us his Spirit so he can dwell within us. Now we are to be the temple of the living God. He has become one of us so that we can become brothers and sisters to him and sons and daughters to his Father. A sense of identification and intimacy with God, latent in the covenant before Christ came, now through Christ becomes every believer's privilege.

This new relationship does not lead to easy or casual intimacy. The Father is still the Holy One, the righteous Judge. The God of Bethlehem, the upper room, and Calvary is the same God as the God of Sinai. There will still be a final judgment, but the Father has appointed another to judge in his place. He has assigned that task to his Son, and so the one before whom every human person will appear is none other than Jesus, who is a human being too. The eternal Judge will be one who has been where we are, who wears flesh just as we do. He is the eternal Son of God, but he is also our brother. God recognizes the differences between God and humans but sacrificially closes that distance. In fact, God wants humanity to share in the communion of love that is the inner life of God. That does not come easily.

The reason for the incarnation, the reason Christ came, was that God does not want to dwell at a distance from us. He wants that distance closed. For that to happen something must make it possible for self-centered human creatures to become comfortable in the presence of a holy God. People must become participants in God's own self-sacrificing holy-love, which necessitates more than a change of conduct. It demands a change of nature as well. That is why the family metaphor is so close to the heart of the relationship. God the Father wants for himself sons and daughters, not just servants. He seeks not just a change in our legal status before him, but rather seeks persons in whom flow the same life that flows in him. Pardon is not enough. God wants an internalization of his values and ways that will make us eternally compatible with him. We must be regenerated so that we can be comfortable in our new family and reciprocate the love the Father extends to us. Jesus shows us the desire that God has for other sons and daughters. We are to be related to the Father as Jesus was.

But the Father wants more than sons and daughters for himself. When he created humankind he had an additional purpose in mind: he sought a spouse for his Son. Only earth's two most intimate relationships—family and marriage—can image God's plan. These divine intentions are made clear in the teachings of Jesus, the Gospels, and the rest of the New Testament. The gospel makes it very clear that the reason for the incarnation and atonement was to prepare us for just such communion with God.

Implicit in the teachings of Jesus, then, is the potential for intimate compatibility between the Holy One and every single one of his human creatures. The highest compliment ever given to human mortals is manifest in God's purposes for us, which are inherent in the teachings of Jesus. The "whosoever" of Jesus means that no one is incapable of a relationship with God; God finds each person infinitely desirable. Therefore, when he made us, he made us for himself, capable of a relationship of perfect love. He pursues us all with love. In fact, he desires us more than we can desire him.

Why does God place such a premium on us and the prospect of our entering into his own common life? Our value and our purpose are not inherent but result from the very nature of the one who made us. He who made us is love; therefore, the works of his hands are objects of his love. This is illustrated in the term God uses to describe his people in Exodus 19:5: "treasured possession." This is a tender Hebrew term that speaks of an object of beauty, value, and special delight. God has not brought them out of Egyptian slavery simply so they can be free. Nor has he brought them to Canaan so they can live their lives in plenty. God has brought them *to himself*: "I carried you on eagles' wings and brought you to myself" (19:4). This is a love story, and the measure of Israel's worth lies not in Israel itself, but in the divine lover's heart. When John says, "God so loved the world," he is telling us first of all about God, but he is also saying something about us. God loves us because he is love, and that love gives us eternal worth because his is an eternal love.

Therefore, it is possible for us to participate in other-oriented, self-giving love, which is the inner life of God himself. When he created us, he made us for companionship with deity. He wants to know us and us to know him. That is why the Genesis account says we were made in the actual image of God with the capacity to respond in freedom to divine overtures of love. God seeks those who will freely choose to love him. He wants those who will actually *like* him enough to enjoy the company of the Father, the Son, and the Holy Spirit.

This brings us to another radical step in our understanding of God. He is one, the Holy One, the single Sovereign, and the Creator out of nothing of all that exists except himself. Human beings are not God, nor can they ever be. Neither are humans capable of becoming holy on their own. So when humanity could not become God, God decided to become a man. God's eternal Son became one of us so that we might become a part of the communion that goes on in the inner nature of God. In Christ we may be participants in that other-oriented, self-giving, holy-love, which is God's being. The God whom Jesus images for us obviously likes us and wants us to be near him, nearer than we ever could have dreamed.

The depth and the richness of the intimacy God seeks to have with us are so profound that no single human metaphor is adequate to express it. As a result, we find three metaphors that are universally present either implicitly or explicitly in the biblical revelation, that in unique fashion indicate how passionately God loves us and wants to draw us into oneness with himself. The first arises out of God's role in his creation as sovereign and righteous judge, the second from the familial relationship of the first and second persons of the Trinity, and the third from the Father's eternal purpose to find a bride for his Son through human history. The next chapter will give us the biblical picture of how these three metaphors are developed in revelation and history.

THE LEVEL OF INTIMACY GOD DESIRES

THREE METAPHORS ILLUSTRATE GOD'S PURPOSES FOR US

The intimacy God seeks with his human creatures is dramatically evidenced for us in the metaphors used to describe our relationship to him. Three are developed extensively throughout Scripture.

THE ROYAL/LEGAL METAPHOR

This first metaphor has for us moderns a double meaning. While it speaks of the royal court where the sovereign reigns, it also speaks of the legal assembly where law reigns and judicial decisions are made. In our society with its separation of powers, we do not think of these two together. However, in the world of the Old Testament, the world in which Israel existed, the sovereign was the supreme judge. God was seen as both King and Judge. He was the giver of the Law and the guarantor of its execution. He was responsible for justice as well as order. He was the Protector of the weak and the inescapable Judge of those who did evil. Sovereign power and legal power were one in Yahweh. The Davidic court and others in the ancient Near East reflected such a union. Particularly in the West, we have learned through bitter experience that, in our fallen state, no mortal can be trusted with both responsibilities. This has produced what we speak of as the "separation of powers," where no person is the law, not even a royal leader, president, or prime minister. In this respect our earthly world does not reflect the eternal one, where sovereignty and justice are united. Since God is one and one alone, the divine throne and the divine bench coincide. The eternal Lord and the eternal Judge are the same.

The Old Testament, particularly the book of Psalms, picks up this theme of Yahweh's kingship and develops it extensively. Psalms 93:1–2 and 99:1–5 are illustrative:

> *The LORD reigns, he is robed in majesty;*
> *   the LORD is robed in majesty*
> *   and is armed with strength.*
> *The world is firmly established;*
> *   it cannot be moved.*
> *Your throne was established long ago;*
> *   you are from all eternity.*

> *The LORD reigns,*
> *   let the nations tremble;*
> *he sits enthroned between the cherubim,*
> *   let the earth shake.*
> *Great is the LORD in Zion;*
> *   he is exalted over all the nations.*
> *Let them praise your great and awesome name—*
> *   he is holy.*
> *The King is mighty, he loves justice—*
> *   you have established equity;*
> *In Jacob you have done*
> *   what is just and right.*
> *Exalt the LORD our God*
> *   and worship at his footstool;*
> *   he is holy.*

This theme is developed in many ways in the Old Testament. One of the tender ways is that of Yahweh as shepherd. The ancient Eastern kings were looked upon as shepherds of their people, responsible for the welfare of their subjects. Yahweh is portrayed as the shepherd king who wants his people to sit at his royal table and dwell in his house forever. Psalm 23 is the classic statement of this. And, David, the shepherd king, becomes the preeminent prefiguring of the coming Messiah.

But Yahweh as king is also the eternal Judge. He is the guarantor that righteousness and justice will ultimately prevail in his cosmos. That is why Abraham could expostulate in the light of the imminent destruction of Sodom and Gomorrah with its possibility that some of the righteous would perish with the unrighteous, "Will not the Judge of all the earth do right?" (Gen. 18:25). This faith in Yahweh as the royal Judge was a source of holy fear in the devout Israelite, but it also gave a sense of security in the face of life's evils. The one who believed was assured that right would ultimately prevail, that Yahweh's own righteousness was the guarantee. Note the confidence of the writer of Psalm 96:

> *Say among the nations, "The LORD reigns."*
> *The world is firmly established, it cannot be moved;*
> *he will judge the peoples with equity.*
> *Let the heavens rejoice, let the earth be glad.*
>
> *... they will sing before the LORD, for he comes,*
> *he comes to judge the earth.*
> *He will judge the world in righteousness*
> *and the peoples in his truth. (vv. 10–11, 13)*

This theme is developed in the New Testament in terms of "the kingdom of God." In announcing the Messiah, John the Baptist insisted that with the king came the kingdom, that it was already "at hand." Jesus himself often used royal language in his preaching, particularly in his parables. How often his disciples heard him say these words: "The kingdom of heaven is like ..."

Paul used royal language as well. Typical of the account of Paul's ministry in the book of Acts is the report that Paul declared the kingdom of God. When he went to Ephesus he "entered the synagogue and spoke boldly there for three months, arguing persuasively about the kingdom of God" (19:8). When he reached Rome he met with the leaders of the

Jewish community, and "From morning till evening he explained and declared to them the kingdom of God and tried to convince them about Jesus" (28:23).

The book of Revelation finally and quite dramatically concludes the biblical data on God as King and Judge. All of creation is pictured as standing before the throne of God. In the center of that throne stands none other than Jesus, who is now recognized as Lord and Judge. Every knee is bent to him in acknowledgment of his sovereign lordship as all creation awaits his judgment. Every creature faces its Creator Judge.

This metaphor provides the context for the development of the doctrine of justification by faith. Humans are seen as God's creatures who have violated the divine law and stand eternally condemned. Salvation is thus needed for deliverance from that seemingly inevitable negative judgment. The good news is that escape has been provided through Christ, who in his passion took the penalty for our sins upon himself and satisfied divine justice. Through acceptance of his sacrifice and through faith in Christ we can stand forgiven and redeemed. Our salvation rests not on what we have done, but on the divine judicial decree that has its basis in what Christ has done for us in the cross. Salvation is not our achievement but God's free, gracious gift to those who believe.

This truth sparked the Reformation. Even a superficial reading of Luther will give one a sense of the power of this truth. Justification by faith became the battle cry of Protestantism, the basis on which most Protestant scholars were inclined to develop their soteriology. This doctrine was a legitimate development of the royal/legal metaphor. Augustine had helped lay the foundation with his concern for the unity of God. He was much clearer in his understanding of God's oneness, his being, than of the nature of personhood in the triune God.

The royal/legal metaphor, however, is only one metaphor Scripture gives us for understanding God's work of redemption. If we view Christ's saving work only in terms of a legal change of status for the sinner, this handles the problem of the sin's penalty but gives no answer to the problem of human sin. Justification then means "to *declare* righteous," not "to *make* righteous."

A classical example of using the legal metaphor in isolation from the others is seen in the work of the Reformed theologian Louis Berkhof. To Berkhof, justification is a legal act of God that "does not affect the condition but the state of the sinner." Speaking from his understanding of Reformed faith, he insists that this legal act "applies to all sins, past, present, and future, and therefore includes the removal of all guilt and of every penalty." It is an act that "does not admit of repetition."[1] In other words, justification is an answer to the problem of the consequences of my sins but not my sinfulness. Righteousness is imputed but not necessarily imparted to the believing sinner. A lost legal position is restored, yet the problem of a rebellious or a divided heart is not adequately addressed. More than imputed righteousness is required if one is to walk joyously in fellowship with the Holy One.

The Reformed understanding of justification has heavily influenced biblical studies in Protestant circles since the Reformation. The result is that the Protestant understanding of salvation has been seen primarily in terms of this Reformed interpretation of the book of Romans. This interpretation of Paul has largely dominated the scene to the neglect of other biblical writers, particularly John, and the basic human problem for soteriology has been laid out in terms of the Law. In Romans, just as in Galatians, the human model that is lifted up as the prime example of justification is Abraham. The irony is that Abraham had no knowledge of the Law. Paul himself acknowledges that the Law, as he wrestled with it, was not a part of Abraham's world and did not come until Moses (see particularly Rom. 5:20).

Yet Abraham had a very intimate personal relationship with God, who later revealed himself at Sinai in a legal covenant. Note Abraham's sacrifice of family, home, and civic security to keep company with Yahweh. Note also his refusal to doubt the promise of his divine friend across a quarter of a century of waiting and wandering. One gets the impression that Abraham's relationship was with Yahweh himself, not primarily with Yahweh's commands. It was more a relationship with promise than with law. The failure of Israel to understand the difference between relating to God himself and relating to God's law lay at the heart of Paul's charges against Israel in his Roman letter, a failure that ultimately led to Israel's rejection of the Messiah. For Paul, Abraham is the prime picture of the justified person, so one gets the feeling that justification for him includes more than a change of legal status.

The royal/legal metaphor is certainly a basic biblical metaphor crucial to our understanding of the gospel. But it is not the only metaphor. Even a casual reading of the Bible will reveal significant portions where other metaphors enrich and illuminate our insight about the communion God seeks with his creatures. Each metaphor has its own logic and its own demands. Each one casts a different light on what the incarnation and atonement are all about. We need the entire biblical witness to see the full richness of the salvation God has provided for us in the cross.

THE FAMILIAL METAPHOR

A second metaphor is the familial one. This metaphor begins early in the Old Testament and develops slowly until it reaches center stage in the life and teaching of Jesus. When God called Moses to liberate the descendants of Abraham from Egyptian bondage, he instructed him to tell Pharaoh to let Yahweh's "son" go. Yahweh speaks of Israel as his "firstborn son" (Ex. 4:22–23). Clearly, God sees his family as extending someday beyond Israel's borders. Israel is to be the door through which other children ultimately may be brought to him. Thus, God's call to Moses is a development of the promise to Abraham that through him all the nations of the earth would find blessing.

Yahweh sees his relationship to Israel as a familial one. This is confirmed in the story of the destruction of the firstborn sons of Egypt on the night of the Passover. It was a matter for Yahweh of firstborn in exchange for firstborn. Little wonder that we find Moses at the end of his life pleading with Israel in these terms:

> Is this the way you repay the LORD,
>   O foolish and unwise people?
> Is he not your Father, your Creator,
>   who made you and formed you? (Deut. 32:6)

Yahweh's relationship with Israel is a very tender one. Note the emotional speech of Yahweh in Hosea:

When Israel was a child, I loved him,
    and out of Egypt I called my son.
But the more I called Israel,
    the further they went from me....
I led them with cords of human kindness,
    with ties of love....

How can I give you up, Ephraim?
    How can I hand you over, Israel? (11:1–2, 4, 8)

What begins as a special relationship to the people of Israel takes a different turn with the appearance of David. The relationship of David to Yahweh and Yahweh to David takes on a unique character, a familial one. The second Psalm, which is considered Davidic and which the New Testament interprets messianically, speaks of the king as Yahweh's own son: "You are my Son; today I have become your Father" (Ps. 2:7). When Yahweh speaks to David about his own son, Solomon, who will succeed David, he says: "I will be his father, and he will be my son" (2 Sam. 7:14). Now it is not just the people of God who are called Yahweh's child, but a single individual, Israel's king.

This is the background for the identification of the throne of David with Israel's messianic hope. That is why the crowd in Jerusalem on Palm Sunday can sing: "Hosanna to the Son of David!" "Blessed is the king who comes in the name of the Lord!" (Matt. 21:9; Luke 19:38). The New Testament insists that the unique relationship David and Jesus share with the Father is now, through Christ, open to all who will believe in him. The Son of God, who is the eternal Son of God the Father, has become a son of David so that all of us who are the children of men might become the children of God.

In fact, Jesus' purpose in the incarnation is that all of God's human creatures might know an eternal relationship with God the Father and the Son that is analogical to the ontological relationship that exists between Father and Son in the triune being of God. So Paul can speak in Romans about our adoption, and John can give us the promise of Jesus himself: "To him who overcomes, I will give the right to sit with me on my throne" (Rev. 3:21). Evidently God who determined that we would all be part of human families intended that those families should image the inner life of God himself and serve as pedagogical devices that would better enable us to understand the intimacy he seeks with us.

A natural consequence of this language is that the Scriptures develop a familial concept of salvation. Thus, we get the biblical teaching on regeneration and the new birth. Nicodemus may have been surprised when Jesus suggested to him that he needed to be born again. The shock came not only in the concept of new birth but in the suggestion that he, a Jew, needed such change. The language of a second birth was the language Judaism used to explain what happened to a Gentile who converted to the faith of Moses. For a Gentile to become a Jew meant entering into a brand-new life, totally discontinuous with his past in the same way Israel's new life with Yahweh after the Exodus was totally distinct from its past. It meant entrance into a new family and a new life. Jesus linked such conversion with the Spirit and spoke of a birth of the Spirit in contrast to the birth in the flesh (John 3:5–8). He was connecting regeneration to a significant Old Testament theme.

A new life of conformity with the will of Yahweh through a new heart brings hope. This is seen in the different figures used in Old Testament writings. The language of circumcision was the sign that one was in a living relationship with Yahweh. In Deuteronomy God begins to promise that he can take away the uncircumcised heart and give a circumcised heart. That new heart will enable us to fulfill Yahweh's desires, that we should love him with all of our hearts and all of our souls (Lev. 26:41; Deut. 10:16; 30:6; Jer. 4:4; 9:25–26). Ezekiel speaks directly of the possibility of a new heart in which the Spirit dwells, enabling the believer to follow Yahweh's decrees (Ezek. 36:24–28). Jeremiah foresees a new covenant where the law will not be written on tablets for the sanctuary but will be placed within Yahweh's people and inscribed on their hearts so that they will know Yahweh (Jer. 31:31–34). All of these prophecies are part of the promise of grace that runs through the Old Testament and finds its fulfillment in the provisions of the cross. It is possible for us through Christ and through the Spirit to be new creatures because we have a new life flowing through us. We have become members of a new family, the family of the one true God. We have a new legal status, but we have more: We are part of a new family. We experience a resurrection to a new life lived in communion with a holy God through the power of the indwelling Holy Spirit.

The idea of new life is the conceptual context in which we must see the references of Jesus to God as his Father. As the people listened to his comments, some, particularly the temple leadership, began to sense that he was speaking for himself of more than a spiritual relationship. They realized that he thought of his relationship as the Son of God to the Father as different from that of David or a devout Jew. He spoke of oneness with the Father, an identity with him, and said and did things that rightfully belonged only within the province of God's authority. He also accepted responses reserved for God alone; for example, he permitted the man to whom he had given sight to worship him. When he referred to himself as the Son of God, he was speaking of a relationship to God that others did not experience when they called God their Father (John 8:41). His insistence that he was not of this world and that he had come as the "sent one" from the Father simply intensified their conviction. They had no categories to handle such comments as, "Before Abraham was born, I am" (John 8:58) – nor his resurrection! Thomas surely could not have justified his exclamation theologically a week later when he cried out, "My Lord and my God!" but he knew there was no other appropriate response (John 20:28).

Left to work their way through the implications of Jesus' references to his relationship to God as his Father, the church fathers concluded that the parent-child relationship, which they had felt was a rich way of explaining how persons were related to God, was really an ontological reality in the case of Christ. This meant that in the very being of God himself, one finds a relationship that is the prototype for all of the family relationships of all of the descendants of Adam. In other words, they became convinced that in Jesus Christ they had not just met a human being in whom God dwelt; rather, in Jesus Christ they had met a person who was himself divine. They had met more than a godly man. They had met one who called himself the Son of God and who, when he said "Father," meant something different than what they meant and experienced when they prayed, "Our Father." Paul was obviously thinking some of these thoughts when he wrote to his Ephesian friends, "For this reason I kneel before the Father, *from whom his whole family* in heaven and on earth derives its name" (Eph. 3:14–15, emphasis added). The term *Father* when used of God has a double thrust.

Therefore, we conclude that in terms of parent-child relationships, God is not like us but we are like God. The full implications of this cannot be developed here. But at least we can make two observations. First, the roots of the family ultimately are in neither biology nor sociology but in theology. Second, the family cannot be explained primarily in human terms; it requires divine categories. If we would fully understand this sociological institution, we must see it in terms of the nature of God and the eternal purposes of God. He made a creation in which every person who ever lived or will live knows what it means to be someone's child or someone's parent or both. To be human means that one has a father. Consider the possibility that every human person is a member of a family with earthly parents because our heavenly Father wills that every human person know him as Father and become a member of his family.

What does this say about the desire in the heart of God for intimacy with us? That we should be servants of God, subjects in his eternal kingdom, is not enough. He wants a closer, more personal relationship, one based not simply on law but one that arises from a shared, common spiritual life. This is a much more intimate and existential relationship than that of a subject with his sovereign. So we must define *salvation* very differently in this context than in terms of the royal/legal metaphor. It is one thing to pray, "O King" and another to say, "Father." Wesley understood this distinction and never ceased to glory in it.

> *My God is reconciled;*
> *His pardoning voice I hear;*
> *He owns me for His child,*
> *I can no longer fear;*
> *With confidence I now draw nigh,*
> *And, "Father, Abba, Father," cry.[2]*

THE NUPTIAL METAPHOR

The third metaphor is an even more intimate one than that of parent and child. It comes from the closest of all human relationships, that between a man and a woman who are bound together in the sacred covenant of matrimony. The most graphic and commonly known biblical imaging of this is found in the life of the prophet Hosea. Yahweh instructs Hosea: "Go, take to yourself an adulterous wife and children of unfaithfulness, because the land is guilty of the vilest adultery in departing from the LORD" (1:2). Yahweh couches his covenantal relationship to Israel in marital terms, and he thinks it appropriate that his representative illustrate in his life the situation in which Yahweh finds himself. Yahweh sees Israel as an unfaithful spouse. He wants his prophet to illustrate his pain in his person.

Ezekiel picks up this theme and turns it into a philosophy of history for the people of Israel (Ezek. 16). He pictures Israel as the child of an Amorite father and a Hittite mother who was cast into the wilderness by her parents and left alone to die. Yahweh sees the forsaken child and takes, washes, feeds, clothes, and nurtures her. When the child reaches the age of love, Yahweh chooses her for his own bride and claims her for himself. Yahweh's comment is: "And you became mine" (16:8; cf. Ex. 19:4; Song 2:16). Nevertheless, Israel had a wandering heart and gave herself to other lovers. From Ezekiel's point of view, the Sinai covenant was a marital covenant, and Israel's election was to be understood in nuptial terms. Because we believe the text is inspired, we recognize that what is being said is not the point of view of the prophet but that of Yahweh himself.

Likewise, Jeremiah speaks of God's election of Israel in tender marital terms. He does not develop the metaphor as Ezekiel did, but it still serves as his frame of reference:

"*I remember the devotion of your youth,*
how as a bride you loved me
and followed me through the desert ...
Israel was holy to the LORD." *(Jer. 2:2–3)*

Isaiah reflects the same paradigm for understanding the relationship of Yahweh to Israel:

No longer will they call you Deserted,
    or name your land Desolate.
But you will be called Hephzibah,
    and your land Beulah;
For the LORD will take delight in you,
    and your land will be married.
As a young man marries a maiden,
        so will your sons marry you;
as a bridegroom rejoices over his bride,
        so will your God rejoice over you. (62:4–5)

The Hebrew makes this passage all the more poignant because *Hephzibah* is the Hebrew for "My delight is in her." *Beulah* in Hebrew means "married," so this land of Beulah, the "promised land," is "a married land."

This way of thinking about Yahweh's relationship to Israel began much earlier than with the prophets. This is seen in the use of the language of idolatry and adultery from Israel's earliest days as a nation in covenant with Yahweh. The marriage metaphor so permeated Israel's thought that it determined the Old Testament's usage of the words for *adultery* and *harlotry.* Israel's disobedience is seen not only as breaking a legal code, but as a violation of a personal marriage covenant. Idolatry is described in terms of adultery and harlotry so commonly that whenever we find these words, we must check whether they refer to sexual practices or spiritual relationships. Adultery is common as a synonym for Israel's idolatrous ways, but idolatry does not occur as a synonym for sexual improprieties!

Israel's worship of gods other than Yahweh is early described as prostitution. In Exodus 34:15 Yahweh describes the worship of idols by Israel's neighbors in terms of prostitution (see also Lev. 17:7; 20:5). So when God appears to Moses before his valedictory to Israel, we are told: "The LORD said to Moses: 'You are going to rest with your fathers, and these people will soon *prostitute* themselves to the foreign gods of the land they are entering. They will forsake me and break the covenant I made with them'" (Deut. 31:16, emphasis added).

Therefore, we must look at the covenant scene at Sinai in Exodus 19–20 not just in legal/political terms. The covenant into which Israel is entering has legal characteristics, but it is much more. From God's perspective it is primarily nuptial. God is taking a bride. The affirmation of Yahweh, as I have suggested before, takes on a great personal tenderness: "You yourselves have seen what I did to Egypt, and how I carried you on eagles' wings and brought you *to myself*" (Ex. 19:4, emphasis added).

Most Old Testament scholars understand what happened at Sinai in terms of the ancient Near Eastern suzerainty covenants. This is not improper. However, it is also legitimate to raise the question of how Yahweh himself thought of this relationship. We do not determine the character of Yahweh by the common understandings of deity in that ancient world. Nor should we limit our understanding of the covenant of Yahweh with Israel by equating it with the extant covenants between other people groups and their gods or their sovereigns. We should look at the relationship of Yahweh to Israel established at Sinai from the perspective of the nature of Yahweh as he is understood by the prophets, by Jesus, and by the New Testament.

In his treatment of Isaiah 54, William Dumbrell seems to concur with our understanding. The prophet Isaiah is speaking a word of hope to Zion in her exile.

> "Do not be afraid; you will not suffer shame. . . .
> You will . . . remember no more the reproach of your widowhood.
> For your Maker is your husband—
> the LORD Almighty is his name—
> the Holy One of Israel is your Redeemer;
> he is called the God of all the earth.
> The LORD will call you back
> as if you were a wife deserted and distressed in spirit—
> a wife who married young,
> only to be rejected," says your God.

"For a brief moment I abandoned you,
      but with deep compassion I will bring you back.
In a surge of anger
      I hid my face from you for a moment,
but with everlasting kindness
      I will have compassion on you,"
      says the LORD your Redeemer. (54:4–8)

Dumbrell comments:

We learn in these verses of a widowed mother, the wife of Yahweh's youth, and of the reproach of her youth, which seems to
have been the period before the call of Israel in Egypt. The
shame of her widowhood seems to be a direct reference to the
exile. Zion, in whom the hopes for Israel have been gathered
together, is depicted as a woman who was espoused in her
youth, cast off because of her sin, but then recalled to the status of a wife. In this personification is a direct reference to Sinai
since marriage is a frequent prophetic metaphor for the
covenant (especially in Jeremiah and Hosea).[3]

This thinking of Yahweh's relationship to Israel in nuptial terms
was taken for granted by the New Testament writers and not explained
on the assumption that the reader would understand. This first becomes
obvious in the story of John the Baptist. His disciples saw that the
crowds following their master were now beginning to follow Jesus.
John's disciples were concerned that Jesus' disciples were baptizing
more disciples than John. They raise a question about this with their
master. Note John's response:

A man can receive only what is given him from heaven. You
yourselves can testify that I said, "I am not the Christ but am
sent ahead of him." The *bride* belongs to *the bridegroom*. The
friend who attends *the bridegroom* waits and listens for him,
and is full of joy when he hears *the bridegroom's* voice. That
joy is mine, and it is now complete. He must become greater;
I must become less. (John 3:27–30, emphasis added)

In other words, John understood his relationship to Jesus as that of a best man to his bridegroom friend. He viewed the mission of Christ in nuptial terms. Perhaps the most impressive thing about this passage is that the author makes no attempt to explain his use of this metaphor. He expects his readers to be thoroughly familiar with it.

Jesus uses the same figure to explain himself. All three of the Synoptics give us the story of people coming to Jesus to ask him why his disciples did not fast. They noted that John's disciples and the disciples of the Pharisees made it a pattern to fast but his disciples did not. Jesus' response makes it clear that the nuptial character of Israel's election determined his understanding of his own mission: "How can the guests of *the bridegroom* fast while he is with them? They cannot, so long as they have him with them. But the time will come when *the bridegroom* will be taken from them, and on that day they will fast" (Mark 2:19–20, emphasis added).

We should not be surprised, then, that John presents the wedding at Cana of Galilee as the beginning of the miracles ("signs") of Jesus' public ministry. The redemption of the world began with a wedding feast and will end with the wedding of Christ and his church. This should help us understand what Jesus meant when he began a parable with, "The kingdom of heaven is like a king who prepared a wedding banquet for his son" (Matt. 22:2).

The last six chapters of the book of Revelation give us the climax of the nuptial metaphor. The royal/legal metaphor is also present in Revelation:

> *Hallelujah!*
> *For our Lord God Almighty reigns.*
> *Let us rejoice and be glad*
> *and give him glory! (19:6–7)*

But the next line–the climax–is this:

> *For the wedding of the Lamb has come,*
> *and his bride has made herself ready.*
> *Fine linen, bright and clean,*
> *was given her to wear. (19:7–8, emphasis added)*

We are given a brief picture of the final judgment (20:4, 11–15), and then we see the New Jerusalem coming down out of heaven "prepared as a bride beautifully dressed for her husband" (21:2). One of the seven angels says, "Come, I will show you the bride, the wife of the Lamb" (v. 9). Not surprisingly, we find a final invitation to salvation: "The Spirit and the bride say, 'Come!' And let him who hears say, 'Come!' Whoever is thirsty, let him come" (22:17). The human story that began with a wedding comes to its end; the wedding in the garden of Eden and every other wedding in human history, including the one at Cana in Galilee, prefigured this end – a royal wedding – the one in which the Father gives a bride to his Son.

Intriguingly, the human social institution we call marriage was in Yahweh's mind before the creation of the world and was devised as a divine pedagogical tool to teach human creatures what human history is really all about. Perhaps the most poignant element in Revelation's picture of the conclusion of history is the introduction to the story of the fall of Babylon in chapter 17. Babylon is the alternative to Israel, the other people of the earth who are not Yahweh's people. The sin that brings her to destruction is described as adultery (18:3, 9). The supreme sign of the judgment of God upon her is described in the same terms Jeremiah used: "The voice of bridegroom and bride will never be heard in you again" (v. 23; cf. Jer. 7:34; 16:9; 25:10; 33:10–11). Symbol and reality are related so closely that when the reality vanishes, its symbols also disappear.

The charge of adultery against Babylon clearly suggests that Yahweh also desired Babylon to be in a nuptial relationship with him. One could conclude that God originally intended to have a nuptial relationship with all of his human creatures. The creation covenant itself was in at least some measure a covenant of love.

Such logic inevitably raises interesting questions about human sexuality. It would appear that Yahweh, who made us all male and female, had distinct pedagogical purposes in mind when he made us sexually differentiated beings. The purposes of God affect our lives in two ways at the most intimate level.

First, it has often been assumed that the primary purpose of human sexuality is procreation. The Old Testament sees children as blessings from God. God obviously is pleased when we reproduce ourselves. His first instruction to the first couple was to be fruitful, to multiply, and to fill the earth (Gen. 1:28). The psalmist tells us:

> *Sons are a heritage from the LORD,*
> *children a reward from him....*
> *Blessed is the man*
> *whose quiver is full of them. (127:3, 5)*

The ancient world tended to see marriage as a means to secure an heir, and it valued a woman by her success in producing an heir. However, it is highly significant that the Song of Songs with its canticles of love never mentions children anywhere. Children do not seem at all necessary to justify the validity and sanctity of nuptial love; they are not to be the purpose of love but its marvelous by-product.

Second, the question for most of us–and a perpetually perplexing one for scholars–relates to the location of the mark of the covenant (circumcision). This mark, which indicated that a man was in covenant relation with Yahweh, was placed on the most private part of the body. The female carried no such mark, but the fact that the sign was at the point where bride and groom meet may have something to say theologically. Human sexuality's biblical origin does not seem to lie in biology. Instead, the source is found in the eternal pedagogical purposes of God, who made all of us either male or female.

Human sexuality is a far more sacred thing for God's followers and a far more significant thing in God's eyes than most of us have dreamed. Perhaps this is why Yahweh takes our sexual conduct so seriously. This leads us once more to the especially intriguing word *holy* (*qadesh* in the Old Testament). Holy is particularly and uniquely Yahweh's word. His claim on the word seems to have implications for his claim on human sexuality as well. God's purpose for coming to us in Jesus is to restore true sanctity to those holy things that humanity has corrupted, sexuality among them.

Human sexuality becomes Paul's key to understanding the church as the body of Christ: Christ is the groom, and the church is Christ's bride. In Ephesians 5:22–33 Paul addresses the question of how a husband should relate to his wife. He insists that Christ has given the supreme example in the cross: the love expressed in his self-sacrifice is God's picture of the love a husband should have for his wife. The cross is the great expression of Christ's love for his bride. Then Paul introduces what seems to be a second metaphor, that of the body: the church as the body of Christ. It is clear that Paul is referring to Genesis 2:21–25 when he quotes Genesis 2:24: "For this reason a man will leave his father and mother and be united to his wife, and the two will become one flesh." So the metaphor of marital reality is primary in explaining the nature of the church.

The writer of the book of Revelation reveals the same marital metaphor when he pictures the end of human, earthly history. The final scene in chapters 19–22 pictures the coming of the *eschaton* in terms of the fulfillment of the promise implicit in Exodus 19–20. The climax of the story of redemption is the marriage supper of the Lamb (Rev. 19:9–10). If history began with a wedding in Eden and closes with one in the New Jerusalem, the biblical story runs from wedding to wedding, from temporal symbol to eternal reality.

IMPLICATIONS OF THE THREE METAPHORS
Royal/Legal Metaphor

From the preceding text we see that the Scriptures use three major metaphors to express the kind of relationship God wants with his creatures. The first is royal/legal. This image is rooted in the political character of human existence, where we find so much of our own identity and security. In that political domain we find who we are and who others are in terms of basic legal rights and responsibilities. Personhood in this sense is a legal concept, because our citizenship is defined as rights and responsibilities in a national entity. So we have membership in one or both of two kingdoms—our earthly citizenship and/or our kingdom citizenship—through the legal act of justification by faith, which makes us acceptable members of God's own kingdom. And the two kingdoms are analogous to each other.

The Familial Metaphor

The second metaphor is familial. We must not overlook the obvious fact that God designed his world so that every human, without exception, has a father and a mother. To be human is to have parents and family relationships from which we get our name and our nature. Legal identity is one thing, but family identity is quite another. In the family we learn who we are and how we are to be, not just as a legal person, but as a human person. We learn how to relate with intimacy to others.

In the state we find first, what our rights and those of others are before the law and second, the definition of our legal responsibilities to others and their responsibilities to us. The emphasis is on equality and legal accountability. In the family a very different sense of right and responsibility reigns. The emphasis is not on equality–that is assumed–but on personal obligation, respect, and love. Here we develop our moral and ethical sensitivities.

For instance, the Decalogue does not command us to obey our parents, but to honor them. The Hebrew word for *honor* is the same word (*kabbed*) that is used when we are told to "glorify" God. This is appropriate in that our parents are the human symbols in our lives of the eternal Father. We should give them respect analogical to that which is due God. This is more than obedience because the primary concern in the family goes much deeper than performance. Our parents are not gods, nor are they supposed to try to act out such a role. They are God's symbols in that they are his agents in giving us life and nurture, and they are the models that are to teach us about God and to point us to him. We are to honor and treat them with respect because of what they symbolize.

The emphasis is not on rights, but on something much more personal, because the family institution has a sanctity that the state does not. Obedience to the law is all that can be required by the state. The pardoned person can hate the judge without violating the law. However, no proper parent is ever content with simple obedience, nor should the child be. Performance in the family should reflect internalized values. A much deeper existential involvement is demanded. Self-giving love should reign. The rule should not be what is due, but what is needed. The members of the family should belong to one another in a way that the state can neither demand nor understand. Need becomes opportunity, not requirement.

The family is not, as we have said, just a sociological institution or a by-product of our biology; it is a divine mystery. The origin of the family lies in the nature of God, who was a family before the first man and woman met. "Father" is the best description of the character and nature of the first member of the Holy Trinity. And if Jesus is to be taken seriously, being a child was not first of all a human experience. Jesus knew that relation before his advent at Bethlehem. The creeds ultimately spell this out for us with their insistence that there was never a time when God was not a Father and never a time when his Son was not the Son. When God decided to create us, he made us in his own image; our personhood as child, and perhaps parent, is but an expression of God's image. So the relation of every child to every parent is a reflection of the relationship between the first and the second persons of the Holy Trinity.[4]

To be part of a family also means a mingling of our life with that of others. Conception and birth mean that something of both the mother and the father is found in the child—something more than physical appearance. To be a person one has to begin his or her existence inside another. The life of the person is first of all part of the life of another. Human life is always a gift. Families learn that they carry each other within themselves whether they choose to do so or not. That relationship is never cut with the umbilical cord. It may be repudiated but not obliterated.

There is a sense in which some imaging of the family is to be found in one's personal essence. When God tells us that he wants us to be his children, he is speaking of an incredibly intimate and personal relationship with us, much more personal than the royal/legal one! He speaks of a common life, not just a common citizenship. When Jesus told

Nicodemus that he must be born from above, he was speaking of the possibility of the very life of God coming into him.

The Nuptial Metaphor

The third metaphor, the marital one, speaks of a deeper personal intimacy than even that of the family. It speaks not just of status or origin but of union – not by nature but by personal choice. Others determine our birth and natural origin, our citizenship and our family. Marriage is the result of choice, the sacred expression of the commitment of our maleness and our femaleness. Again, we should not overlook the obvious: everyone we will ever meet is either male or female. Sexual identity is our birthright; we can't escape it. We are distinctly made male or female by divine intent. Genesis tells us that even our differences call to mind the one who made us.

> So God created man in his own image,
>   in the image of God he created him;
>   male and female he created them. (1:27)

Biblically, marriage is the union of two persons in such self-giving love that they share a name, their bodies, their possessions, their vocation, their common life – their total selves. This is supposed to be a picture of the relationship that every believer may have with Christ. At the heart of this marital relationship is the sharing of one's physical body and sexuality with another. This makes marriage unique in that only within marriage is this supposed to be true. One can share time, possessions, influence, friendship, work, and almost everything else with others without necessarily damaging the marriage relationship. For a married person to share his or her body with any other than one's spouse is to violate the covenant that has been established between them. But for *true* lovers, keeping a covenant with each other is no restriction. The very essence of true marital love and the marital relationship is the knowledge that the fulfillment of the normal human person can be found only in such a sacred and exclusive relationship with another of the opposite sex. The character of human jealousy and the sense of betrayal that the wounded party always feels when a spouse

gives himself or herself physically to another is witness to the fact that they were designed to keep themselves only for each other.

Since it was God who created our sexuality, he obviously had pedagogical purposes in making us males and females. The royal/legal metaphor or that of the family cannot convey some of the things we need to learn about the relationship that God desires with us here on earth. His purposes have to do with love, covenantal commitment, and self-giving. Karol Wojtyla, Pope John Paul II, suggests that marriage is God's best way to image for us both Christ's love for us who make up his church and also the self-giving love that characterizes the inner life of the triune God. In fact, Wojtyla speaks of "the iconography of marriage" and describes the relationship of the believing husband and wife as earth's most illuminating icon of self-giving love, earth's closest counterpart to the love that is the inner life of the triune Godhead.[5]

DEVELOPMENT OF THE METAPHORS

The biblical development of these three metaphors should make it clear that God places high value on each of us and seeks a remarkably intimate relationship with us. The invitation he extends to us is to enter into the actual life, fellowship, and love that the three persons of the Godhead share with one another. The divine purpose expressed in that invitation is a key to the true understanding of every aspect of the gospel. For example, when we understand sin in an Edenic context, we see it as that which shattered the covenant implicit within the Creator/creature relationship. We also can see that salvation is God's gift to restore us to fellowship. Christ died to do more than get us past the judgment and help us escape hell. He became incarnate and died on Calvary's cross to remove any impediments that would hinder us from being comfortable in his presence and to change us so we can enjoy him in self-giving love now and forever. Any understanding of the atonement that does not make provision to get us ready for that intimacy with him is inadequate, incomplete, and only partially biblical.

From a biblical perspective human life has a *telic* character about it. Structured by divine pedagogical design, we have categories of human experience in thought and language that prepare us for

understanding God's purposes for us when we are confronted with them. When the Word of God comes to us, it is not a completely alien word. Nor does it come to us in a totally foreign tongue. It is a Word for the kind of people we are, the kind of people whom God created for that very Word. What a wonderful story!

Isaiah understood something of the glory of all this: "Who has believed our message?" (53:l). In other words, "What I have to say to you is well beyond belief ... incredible ... too good to be true." And it is! When we did not want God, God wanted us. When we would not come to God, he came to us. When we resisted him, he plotted to win us. When we could not cross the chasm that separates creation from deity, God decided to cross it and become one of us. He would not give up his deity; rather, he would unite divinity and humanity in a single person so that God and humans would really meet and become one. As I have said, God would wed himself to his creation. Thus, the incarnation.

The difference between the monotheism of Christianity and that of Islam and Judaism now cries out to us. The oneness of God in both Islam and Judaism has no inner differentiation to make such a thing as the incarnation possible. Therefore, the claims of Christ about himself are to Judaism and Islam pure blasphemy. This reveals how central and essential the doctrine of the Trinity is to the Christian faith. What to the world is a contradiction is to the Christian a necessity and a glory, even though it remains a mystery. God can cross the chasm between himself and his creation, and his creation can receive him. The Christian marvels at these two glories: (1) God became a human person, and (2) humankind is made with the capacity for union with such a God! In no other religion but Christianity do we see this potential within humanity. To others it is unthinkable.

Jesus Christ gives us a fully developed picture of God: he is one and one alone. He is without rival or competitor. But in that oneness there is otherness. The otherness is first of all familial–that of Father and Son. The one gives life to the other. And this other is also other-oriented. The other receives life that is actually the very life of the one who is giving, which in its very nature is other-oriented. This means that the relationship of the two is that of self-giving, other-oriented love. And from that love comes a third person, the Spirit.

These three "othernesses" are othernesses of likeness. The *oneness* is ontological; it has to do with being. The otherness is *personal*, not ontological. Their being is one, but their persons are differentiated. The second is called the Son of the Father through the Spirit, and the third we name the Spirit of the Father and of the Son. They exist in a communion that is characterized by reason because it is verbal. So they are of one mind. And they are of one spirit because they share their common life with each other. Two of these persons exist in a familial relationship, and the Spirit is the Spirit of the other two. In other words, one is not thinkable without the others. A. N. Williams, drawing upon Richard of St. Victor, calls this "distinction-in-alterity" or "distinction-in-otherness."[6]

It is difficult to imagine the intellectual effort needed for the church to understand the teachings of Jesus about himself, his Father, and the Spirit. The mental paradigm with which the early Christians had interpreted all reality, a paradigm built on the understanding of God as one without any inner differentiation, was shattered. They found themselves thinking radically new thoughts. Ideas that seemed to them logically contradictory now seemed of necessity wedded and therefore compatible. New concepts began to develop, but no vocabulary was available to adequately express them. So how could they communicate what it all meant? The intellectual challenge was overwhelming. They could not, however, back away from it. The result is what many feel is the most significant advance in human thought in history. Time was required–four hundred years in fact–to refine their thinking, develop appropriate vocabulary, and reduce their conclusions to creedal form. They could not stop until they had done it. Even then they did not see all there was to see. They saw the foundational realities and left to us in subsequent centuries (and we have been slow) to probe more deeply, under the inspiration and leadership of the Spirit, the fuller implications of what has been revealed and what there is to know about God.

PERSONHOOD AND THE CONCEPT OF GOD

If the early Christians were to finish their thinking about God as he had been revealed to them through Christ, they had to take another step.

JESUS REVEALS THE NATURE OF PERSONHOOD

Early Christians knew that God is one, the sovereign Creator of all that exists. They understood that he had brought all into existence by the Word of his mouth *ex nihilo*. The creation cannot exist by itself, but is sustained by the same divine Word through which it was created. Any worth it possesses, like its existence, is the consequence of its relationship to God, a relationship of grace, since existence is a free gift from him. The creature therefore should worship and revere the Creator.

The dependence of all things on the will of the Creator for their very existence does not mean that the creation is a toy in the hands of its Maker. According to the Bible, the creation is an object of divine love and delight. That God is not content with separation and detachment is the source of mystery and wonder. God wants a closeness that means *actual personal identification with the creation*, not an ontological identification. Since the creation cannot cross the chasm to him, God crossed the chasm to it. He did this in the incarnation of his Son, Jesus. The Father asked the Son to take on human flesh and become one with the creation in the person of Mary's boy. In this act God *weds himself to his own creation.* Once this is understood, one can never think of God or the creation in the same way again: God and creation belong to each other in a new and very intimate way. God and man in Christ are joined inseparably. If we could look into the very inner life of the Godhead, we would see one of us, Mary's son! The incarnation not only brought about the possibility of regenerational change for us, but of actual change in the life of the changeless one, God himself!

To grasp the radical nature of the thought that God would take on human flesh, one has only to read the death scene of Socrates, the wisest of the Greeks. According to his friend Phaedo, as Socrates faced death he talked with his close companions about the relationship of the soul and the body. The physical body is, according to his understanding, a prison for the soul that enchains and corrupts the soul. Humanity's greatest freedom comes at the point of release from the shackles of the physical body in death. Therefore, a true philosopher who understands this will spend life looking for ways to find freedom from this corrupting impediment. Deliverance from the material body means liberty for the soul. Thus, Socrates receives with great equanimity the cup of poison that he believes will set him free.

In Greek philosophy the body is something to be lamented. The intelligent person longs for escape from its trammels and pollution. Here is another of those many examples where biblical thought is opposite the so-called wisdom of the world. The early Christians saw the God of the Bible as one who seeks the very thing the Greek philosopher scorns—union with the material world by means of enfleshment. We can see the uniqueness and the wonder of the biblical understanding of creation. When we first read in Genesis how God looked at creation on the sixth day and called it "good–very good," most of us have little notion of how good God felt it really was. The creation carried within it the potential for an unbelievably intimate and eternal relationship with God. It was good enough for permanent union with one of the persons of the Godhead.

To begin to understand this revolutionary paradigm shift, think about the ascension of Jesus. Paul makes it clear that when Jesus came out of the tomb, he came with a body. It was a resurrected body but a body nevertheless. Thomas could touch it, everyone could see it, and it could assimilate a breakfast of fish with no problem. When Jesus ascended he took his body with him. Paul indicates that when Jesus returns he will come in bodily form. No human can be thought of as ultimately distinct from his or her body. We are not primarily immaterial spirits to be saved only partially. Our destiny is to be saved wholly as eternally enfleshed persons. The incarnation and resurrection confirm that. This is so radical a concept that early debates and division in the church centered on it. Docetism surfaced again and again, but the orthodox church continued to reject it because the body is good! Good enough for God to identify with and wear.

Earlier I said that Jesus came to give us an *ad intra* view of the inner life of God. When Mary conceived, the inner life of the "Changeless One" began to change and became accessible to the human heart and mind. The incarnation reveals the heart and essence of God; his absolute essence is unchanging and unalterable. Yet the Word became speechless.

The Creator of the cosmos became a fetus in a young woman's womb, and the Maker of heaven and earth became dependent on a young girl's breasts! If we had eyes to see the inner being of God, we would, as was noted earlier, see someone like ourselves—our brother—the son of Mary. For the Muslim or for the orthodox Jew, the very thought would be blasphemous. For the Christian it is occasion to hide one's face in awe and adoration. Isaiah spoke appropriately when he said, "Who has believed our report?" To the natural person it is clearly unbelievable. The world around us uses the word *god*, but it does not mean this God. Only in the heart of the Christian community can one find a concept of God as holy love, who seeks identity and fellowship with us and who desires union with us to such a degree that he willingly became one of us.

We have already seen how the coming of Jesus began a new and radically different understanding of the nature of God. Moses made it clear that God is one. Yet in that oneness there is otherness, an otherness that has three faces. God is at the same time Father, Son, and Spirit. How was this otherness to be explained? To the early church Jesus and the biblical story made the threeness inescapable. Three historical focal points had to be related and explained: Sinai, Bethlehem, and Pentecost. The immanental Trinity (God as he exists in himself) and the economic Trinity (God as he has revealed himself in history) are the same.

The early Christians could not forfeit their belief in the oneness of God. To do so would be to repudiate their Scriptures. Nor could they deny the distinctions reflected in these three revelatory events. Was the God who revealed himself at Sinai the same God they sensed in Jesus Christ? Was the Spirit who came at Pentecost another and different manifestation of the same God who came to Moses and who was present in the human Jesus? Do we have three different manifestations of the same personal God in all three events?

Later, some Christian leaders would believe that, as children of Abraham, they must insist there is only one God and that Sinai, Bethlehem, and Pentecost were simply moments when the same divine person appeared to men in different modal expressions. Most early church fathers found they could not accept this. They looked to Jesus for a solution to the dilemma. Jesus spoke of God as his Father, distinct from him, the same God as the one who appeared to Abraham and Moses and whom Israel knew as the one God. Yet Jesus identified himself as one with this God and did things that only this God can do (forgive sins, raise the dead, and accept worship!). Jesus claimed and accepted a status that was reserved for the divine. Likewise, he differentiated himself from the Spirit of God while he claimed to be the one who would give the Spirit of God to his followers.

The pagan neighbors of the early church had an easy answer. They insisted that Christians were really like themselves; they had three different gods. This theory, of course, was untenable for the first believers, for they were children of Abraham and Moses. The moral and philosophical conclusions that went with paganism were abhorrent to them. Yet their Jewish friends also found the faith of the early Christians unacceptable. To the Jews, Christians were attributing deity to a human being and thus were guilty of the supreme blasphemy.

Some who encountered the Christians were unwilling to differentiate the Spirit from the Father; they decided that Jesus was a very special creature of God, far higher than the normal human but, nevertheless, a creature. They appealed to Paul's description of Jesus as "the firstborn over all creation" (Col. 1:15). For them Jesus stood in between the human being and the highest divine. Such thinking was common in Greek circles where the thought of "ladders of being" from the lowest type of creature to the highest forms of the divine were seen as a continuous scale of ascent. So some wanted to place Jesus at the highest level on that scale, which could still be called "creature."

The church could not consent to any such proposal. Somehow the oneness of God *and* the distinctions within his being must be maintained, or everything would be lost. There is no salvation for humans outside of God. Jesus was, for them, their only possible means of salvation. Somehow the two must be one. But how?

The central question became, "Who is Jesus?" Was he God? Was he some mediating being from an intermediary world? Or was he just an exceptionally good man? Or, mystery of mysteries, was he both God and man? If so, how? The answering of these questions dominated the attention of the church for its first four centuries. It constituted an intellectual and spiritual adventure that has its only parallel in the revolutionary intellectual breakthrough that came with Moses and the development of Hebrew monotheism.

In fact, the early church's quest for truth is the second act of a two-stage drama of biblical faith. The conclusion, in the words of the Nicene Creed, was that Jesus was "the Son of God, the only-begotten generated from the Father ... God from God, Light from Light, true God from true God ... one in being with the Father.... For us men and for our salvation, he came down, and became flesh, was made man." In other words, Jesus was God and man. But how could this be? The key that unlocked the mystery lay in the development of the concept and the vocabulary of *personhood*.[1]

THE PERSON VS. THE SELF

This concern for personhood is somewhat foreign territory for modern and postmodern thinkers. The reason is that our interest has been not with the *person*, but with the *self*. This emphasis on the self began particularly in Western thought through the work of Augustine. He was convinced that we need to look within to find God, so even his work on the Trinity was largely a study in human psychology. Our interiority was his prime concern. Descartes picked up this concern for interiority in hopes of finding the self. Although a theist, he did not make the search for God his prime interest. He wanted to find his inner self as a separate and isolated object, the initial building block of epistemological certainty. The result was the modern and postmodern search for the self, a search based on the assumption that the isolation of the self might make possible the understanding of the self.

In light of our previous discussion, it is clear that the human self has no subsistence apart from God. It never comes alone. Its very self-definition is found in its relationships with God and with others. Therefore, success—in our search as modern and postmodern people conduct it—is precluded by the direction in which we look. When relationships with God and others are considered, we find that we are images of another and are neither complete nor self-explanatory in ourselves. We are ectypes, analogues, of a prototype from whom we receive our existence, our identity, and our self-definition. To know us alone would not be to know us at all. We need to know the model from which our personal nature was drawn if we are to find out who we are. That model is in the triune Godhead.

The disciples of Jesus knew that in Jesus they had confronted more than a man. They accepted his word that, when they saw him, they were seeing the Father. They believed they had been face-to-face with God. So when they tried to describe who Jesus was, they found themselves using two terms. Those in the East whose language was Greek turned to the term for face, *prosopon*. Those in the West who spoke Latin used the Latin equivalent, *persona*. These words seemed to them to support their conviction that God had come to them in Christ and that in him they had really seen God, as it were, face-to-face.

Unfortunately, there was a problem with these terms. Both of them had an original association with the face; they were both used in the context of the theater to speak of the masks actors wore on stage to indicate which roles they were playing. So both words came to represent *masks.* The early Christians were not comfortable with this definition. Their conviction was that Jesus was no play-actor performing a given role, and that the term *Son* spoke of identity, not just function or act. For the early Christians, there could be no division between being and acting in God, between whom he was and what he was doing. They believed that when they had come to know Christ, they had encountered God himself. They listened to Jesus as he spoke about his Father and accepted the fact that he was not the Father. After all, they had watched him die on the cross, and the universe did not disintegrate with his death. Someone had sustained all things while he was destroyed. They remembered what Jesus had told them about the Spirit and knew that he was not the Spirit. They accepted his identification of himself as the Son and believed that this was no act.

But how could they put each piece of this puzzle together and protect the integrity of each truth? What language could they use? Their only option was to take the language they had and fill its terms with new meaning. Moses had to redefine words like *god, create, holy,* and *salvation.* Now the Christians had to do that with words like *love, grace,* and *person.* Four centuries of hard intellectual effort followed, but the conclusion was the gift to the world of new and revolutionary concepts contained in old verbal attire. As they sought an answer to the question of who Jesus could be, among the most crucial were the development of the whole concept and the language of the *person.* To the early Christians, we owe the words and the concepts so important to the social and psychological sciences of today: *person, personhood, personality,* and *personal.*

What did these early Christians mean when they used the word *person* to speak of the different members of the Trinity? When we use these terms of personhood, we have an immediate point of reference. We tend to make the same mistake that so many of us have made with the word *Father.* Naturally, we start with the word *Father* as descriptive of a human relationship, which we want to use to help us understand God, how to relate to him, and how to explain the divine being. It usually comes as a jolt to us to realize that in Christian thought the word *Father* first applies to the first person of the Holy Trinity and only in an analogical way to human fatherhood; *Father* speaks of the divine reality that helps us know what the human relation should be. Adam was not the first father. The fact is that the divine fatherhood is explanatory of human fatherhood, not human fatherhood explanatory of the divine fatherhood. Until we know the origin of the word *person* in Western thought, we make the same mistake. We think of personhood as a human reality that is helpful in our understanding of God. That thinking must be reversed.

When the early church fathers used the word *person,* their referent was first of all to one of the three persons of the Holy Trinity. Such use as a referent to a human being developed only secondarily. The content of the term *person* for the church was determined by the understanding of the Trinity and, in particular, the nature of the Son. The application to human persons came later and is strictly metaphorical. The fact that the Scriptures teach us that we are made in the image of the Son makes it possible for the terms used to describe the Father, the Son, and the Holy Spirit to be used also to describe us. When this language is used to refer to one of the members of the Holy Trinity, it is used of the original, the divine original of which we are only creaturely likenesses. When it is used of us, it is used analogically.

What, then, is a person? First, the word itself is a symbol for real distinctions within the very being of God. *Person* is used in contrast to the word *being,* which was used to describe the oneness of God, the being that is common to the three persons of the Father, the Son, and the Spirit. When the church fathers spoke of Jesus as the Son, they were speaking of him as divine, but they knew that the Son did not develop completely the nature of God. The Father and the Spirit were divine too. So, to differentiate the Son in the being of God, they chose to describe him as a "person" within the Godhead. Note the language of the Athanasian Creed: "One: not by conversion of the Godhead into flesh: but by taking of the manhood into God ... not by confusion of substance: but by unity of person." Thus, Jesus is the one who gives definition to the term *person* for us. We must look to him and his relationship to the other two persons of the Trinity to establish our understanding of the term we apply to ourselves.

The information that comes from Jesus' comments about his relationship to his Father and to the Spirit is most helpful to us. Here again the Gospel of John is crucial. Similar material in the Synoptics addresses the relationship of Jesus to the Father and to the Spirit, but the Johannine material is much fuller and more detailed. A close look at it makes several conclusions obvious.

THE DEFINITION OF PERSONHOOD

Consciousness of Identity

First, we find in examining the texts of our gospels that Jesus had a *clear consciousness of his own identity* as the Son. He had a clear sense that he was to be distinguished from the Father and the Spirit. He knew who he was: the Son. He realized that he was different from his disciples and that the difference lay in his unique relationship to the Father and the Spirit. As the Son, his Sonship was different from the sonship his disciples knew from within their human families and from the spiritual sonship they knew through the new birth, which they were beginning to understand from his teachings. Jesus' conversation with Nicodemus about the new birth is very significant. Here the Sonship of Jesus is ontological, not spiritual.

Jesus makes his claims to divinity yet is very clear that he is not the Father. When he speaks of the Father, he always speaks of him as other than himself. He likewise acknowledges the individual existence of the Spirit and promises that he himself will give the Spirit to the disciples distinct from himself as a gift. He tells them the Spirit will take his place in their lives. Therefore, he is not identical with the Spirit. Yet he insists that there is oneness with the Father and the Spirit that makes him inseparable from the Father and the Spirit. He has his own distinct and unique individuality. He is not the Godhead. He is one person in that Godhead. If Jesus is an example of a person, then a human person should have a similar awareness of his or her own unique, individual, incommunicable personhood.

Meister Eckhart, a German mystic, wrote:

> *That I am a man,*
> *this I share with other men.*
> *That I see and hear and*

> *that I eat and drink*
> *is what all animals do likewise.*
> *But that I am I is only mine*
> *and belongs to me*
> *and nobody else;*
> *To no other man*
> *not to an angel nor to God*
> *except inasmuch*
> *as I am one with Him.*[2]

Karol Wojtyla insists that one of the key marks of personhood is self-possession, which is another way of referring to a person's incommunicable individuality. This becomes especially significant when we speak of the fact that a person's fulfillment comes only in self-giving love. Individuals cannot give away their selves in self-giving love if they are not first of all in possession of their own selves.[3] Jesus knew his own identity, mission, and purpose; that understanding enabled him to give himself away for other people.

Created for Webs of Relationships

Therefore, if Jesus is the prototype of all other persons, then persons never exist alone, because the Son cannot be explained apart from the Father and the Spirit. He is distinct in himself but inseparable from the Father and the Spirit. He and all other persons always operate in *webs of relationships* because persons, human or divine, by definition do not and cannot stand alone.

The explanation of Jesus as the eternal Son of God and as the son of Mary cannot be found in him alone. He is a part of the being of the triune Godhead and finds his divine identity in those relationships that make up that being. He is also the son of Mary, a Jewess of the lineage of David the king, and his identity as a human is derived from that set of relationships. His very self-definition is in terms of that relatedness. When he explains his relationship to his Father, he makes it clear that he is not self-originating. His origin is not in himself, because he is begotten of the Father. Nor is he self-sustaining. He does not have life in himself. He draws his life from the Father. He is the *eternally being-begotten one.* Nor is he self-explanatory. He is the Son, and a son by definition finds his identity in relation to his father. Nor is he self-fulfilling. He came not to do his own will. He came out of love for the Father to do the Father's will. And his fulfillment is in doing his Father's will, not his own. He participates in the triune life of the Father and the Spirit and draws his origin, life, ministry, and sense of identity from them.

The Gospels are clear about Jesus' relationship with the Holy Spirit. He is conceived by the Spirit, which means that the incarnation of the eternal Son is the work of the third person of the Trinity, the Holy Spirit. In a sense Jesus is the gift of the Spirit to us. Jesus' ministry does not nor cannot begin until he is anointed by the Spirit at his baptism. Immediately thereafter he is led into the wilderness by the Spirit to confront the Devil. He draws strength, insight, and power from the Spirit and comes through that contest victoriously. Jesus acknowledges that the power in his miraculous works comes from the Holy Spirit. By the power of the Spirit, he casts out demons.

Jesus affirms more than once in John's gospel that the words he speaks are not his own. They come from the Father through the Spirit. When he stands to preach for the first time in his home synagogue in Nazareth, he quotes a passage from Isaiah 61. He obviously feels that the Spirit of God rests on him and is the key to his preaching and other good works. He insists that the very words he is preaching come from the Father through the Spirit. The writer of the book of Hebrews puts the capstone on this chain of thought when he says it was through the eternal Spirit that Christ "offered himself unblemished to God" (9:14). Thus his sacrifice of himself on the cross was "through the eternal Spirit."

Therefore, if Jesus is the prototypical person in relation to whom all human persons are simply ectypes, or analogues, it is safe to say that persons never come alone. The concept of the person as the autonomous individual whose identity is found in the self is an Enlightenment notion that finds no support in reality or in biblical thought. The concept has no roots in the original definition of *person.* The modern search for a self in isolation is futile. We moderns have an imperfect understanding of what it means to be a person. We do not understand that persons find themselves in their relationships; therefore, we do not understand what it means to be ourselves.

Created for Reciprocal Relationships

As is obvious from the preceding material about Jesus' relatedness to the Father and the Spirit, the relationships in which Christ finds his identity are *reciprocal*. What is being said about the Son can be said about the other two persons of the Trinity: neither of them stands alone. Through the Son the redemptive will of the Father concerning his creation is accomplished, and that good work is done by the Father in the Son through the Holy Spirit. Persons are uniquely distinct, but they are never independent. They exist in conditions of mutual giving and receiving; not just in the receiving and giving of gifts, but in the giving and receiving of one another. Karol Wojtyla, in describing the nature of God, speaks of the "Law of the Gift" as a controlling concept in understanding persons. Thomas Torrance defines the being of God as a "Being-for-others," which finds its best expression in the interpersonal life of the triune Godhead. The early church fathers were so moved by this sublime insight that they developed their own language for it. They spoke of *perichoresis*.

The term *perichoresis* derives from two Greek words: (1) *chora*, which means "space" or "room" and is the nominal form of the verb *choreo*, "to make room for"; plus (2) the preposition *peri*, which means "around" or "about." But it came to be used to express how one person can be open to another. Gregory Nazianzus uses *perichoresis* to explain how Jesus could be both God and man simultaneously without diminution of either the divinity or the humanity. He understood the two distinct natures in Christ as *co-indwelling* one another, or as Thomas Torrance would say, one nature *inexisting* co-inherently within the other without the integrity of either nature suffering loss.[4] The Athanasian Creed expresses the idea of *perichoresis* when it says, "One: not by conversion of the Godhead into flesh ... not by confusion of substance: but by unity of person."

John of Damascus then used this term to explain the words of Jesus: "I am in the Father and the Father is in me" (John 14:11). John the Damascene understood the relationship of the Father and the Son and the Spirit as one in which each member indwelt the other two *perichoretically*. As Torrance points out, the term "gave expression to the dynamic Union and Communion of the Father, the Son and the Holy Spirit with one another in one Being in such a way that they have their Being in each other and reciprocally contain one another, without any coalescing or commingling with one another and yet without any separation from the other for they are completely equal and identical in Deity and Power."[5] *Perichoresis* became the linguistic key to the development of the concept of the Trinity and of the personhood of the three different members of the Trinity.

The inner life of the triune Godhead is thus a life of communion in which the three divine persons live from, for, and in one another. This concept implied a completely new perspective on what it means to be a human person. In Jesus, we confront both the eternal Son of God and Mary's son. Jesus was not only divine; he was, and is, human. In showing us what an original divine person is, he also revealed what a human person was meant to be and–through Christ's atoning sacrifice–can be. As Paul would say, he is the second Adam, the last Adam, the true Adam.

Thus, persons are always found in webs of relationships. The relationships are reciprocal, a matter of giving and receiving. Persons draw their lives from others and find their fulfillment in giving themselves to one another. The philosopher Gabriel Marcel spoke movingly about self-giving in his Gifford Lectures of 1949–50. He said that it is in "intersubjectivity" that we know ourselves and our world. He sees much of modern thought as too Cartesian, resulting in egocentrism or "being-for-itself" that cuts us off from others; in cutting ourselves off from others, we cut ourselves off from ourselves. "A complete and concrete knowledge of oneself cannot be heauto-centric [self-centered]; however paradoxical it may seem, I should prefer to say that it must be hetero-centric [other-centered]. The fact is that we can understand ourselves by starting from the other, or from others, and only by starting from them."[6] Marcel's witness as a philosopher indicates that the data to support this understanding of personhood is not derived from divine revelation alone. Rather, Jesus is the evidence that abounds and flourishes as the most rational explanation of what it means to be a human person.

Characterizing the original persons was reciprocity of love. Jesus tells us that his love relationship to the Father and the Spirit is not something that God does, but what he is (1 John 4:8, 16). This is simply another way of speaking of the *perichoretic*, co-inherent life that the three persons of the Godhead enjoy with one another. That divinely reciprocal life is the source from which all persons come. The personhood of the three members of the Godhead makes that life possible. Their personhood is the prototype of all personhood, and God's personhood creates in order to extend relationality. Our human personhood is the image of divine personhood no matter how disfigured through sin we have become through our "being-for-ourselves."

Created to Be Free

A fourth characteristic of personhood as seen in Jesus is *freedom*, a conclusion we draw from listening to and observing Jesus. His life on earth was one of submission to his Father. He did not come to do his own will. He came to do fully the will of his Father. Yet he makes it clear that his Father's will was not imposed on him. His path of submission was freely chosen. He found fulfillment in doing the will of his Father. It was his delight, as well as his chosen duty, and he found no conflict between the two. He was free, and he longed for everyone else to experience the freedom he enjoyed (John 8:36).

Freedom does not make Jesus independent in the sense that he has a life separate from the Father. His life comes to him from his Father. He is free in his Father's love. The relationship of Jesus to the Father is illustrated dramatically in Jesus' use of three prepositional phrases. They are synonymous although different in their verbal expression. One is the phrase "from myself" (*ap' emautou*). This is used when he is speaking of himself in the first person. The second is "from [out of] himself" (*ex heautou*), which he uses of himself when he is speaking of himself in the third person. The third is "from [out of] myself" (*ex emautou*), a variant of the first phrase. These phrases are found in the passages where Jesus is speaking about the fact that he came to do the will of his Father.

The first occurrence of one of these phrases occurs in Jesus' first alter-cation with the Jewish leaders, recorded in John 5, when he had healed on the Sabbath the man who had been an invalid for thirty-eight years and had told him to carry his pallet. When challenged by the temple lead-ership, Jesus responded by assuring them that he was simply doing the work of his Father; that he could do nothing by himself (*out of himself*); that he could do only what he saw the Father doing (John 5:19).

The second occurrence is at the end of this discourse. Jesus flatly says in verse 30, "*By myself* I can do nothing" (emphasis added). The next occurrence of one of these phrases is again in Jerusalem at the Feast of Tabernacles. The temple leaders are wondering where Jesus got his wisdom since he had never "studied." He assures them that his teaching is not his own, that he does not speak *from himself* (John 7:16). His teaching is from God who sent him. Then he proclaims that one who speaks *from himself* does so to gain honor for himself, a sin of which he is not guilty. A person of truth, he says, works for the honor of the one who sent him (John 7:18). Jesus fits that pattern in that his origin is not in himself; his work and word do not come *from himself*, nor is his end in himself.

In chapter 8 Jesus repeats this claim about his word when the Phar-isees challenge him about his witness. His response is: "I do nothing on my own [*from myself*] but speak just what the Father has taught me" (John 8:28). During that final week in Jerusalem, Jesus returns to this subject. As he approaches the cross, he looks back on his days on earth and considers his teaching. His observation: "For I did not speak of my own accord [*out of myself*], but the Father who sent me commanded me what to say and how to say it" (John 12:49). Alone with his disciples in the upper room the last night before the cross, he returns to this theme: "The words I say to you are not just my own [*from myself*]. Rather, it is the Father, living in me, who is doing his work" (John 14:10).

Significantly, every occurrence of this phrase that we have cited from the Gospel of John is in the negative. Neither Jesus' works nor his words originate from himself. On only one occasion does the phrase appear in a positive frame: in chapter 10 where he is speaking of himself as the Good Shepherd. He says that a good shepherd, in contrast to a hireling, lays down his life for his sheep. This is why he has come, to lay down his life. He says, "No one takes it from me, but I lay it down of my own accord [*from myself*]" (John 10:18). He insists that he has full authority to lay it down and take it up again. His Father has sent him to sacrifice himself. That is his Father's will, and his Father is pleased he is doing it. In fact, his Father loves him because he is doing it. But the choice is his own. No one is making him do it; it is not an imposition. It is a joyous choice because it is right, and it is made freely. It is what a good shepherd should do. The welfare of the sheep is more important to the shepherd than his own well-being. He is the Good Shepherd.

In John 10 we get a revelation of the nature of God that is different—in fact, unique. Really, this is a eucharistic passage. Normally, shepherds keep sheep so they can eat them and wear the wool or sell them so someone else can eat or wear them. Now Jesus tells us about a shepherd who keeps sheep, not so that he can eat or wear or sell them, but so that the sheep can actually eat and wear him. Little wonder the early church heard in this passage an echo of Jesus' paschal words that were later translated into the liturgy of the communion service, in essence: "This is my body. Take, eat, and feed on me within your hearts by faith. This cup is the blood of a new covenant. All of you, drink of it."

Jesus insists that he is not speaking simply of himself. What they see in him is representative of the very nature of God, his Father. This concept of God differs from our prevailing notion. God is not one who seeks those who will give gifts to him. Rather, he seeks those to whom he can give a gift, his very life. Jesus in this passage is simply illustrating what he considers the supreme characteristic of God. Jesus is not living for himself, nor is he choosing for himself. The life he is living is the life that was given to him by the Father, and now he comes to give it to others. But this is not just true of Jesus and his Father. It is also true of the Holy Spirit. In John, Jesus tells us that the Spirit gives himself away as well: "When he, the Spirit of truth, comes, he will guide you into all truth. He will not speak on his own [*from himself*]; he will speak only what he hears, and he will tell you what is yet to come. He will bring glory to me by taking from what is mine and making it known to you. All that belongs to the Father is mine. That is why I said the Spirit will take from what is mine and make it known to you" (John 16:13–15). The Spirit takes what belongs to the Father and the Son and gives it away to us. He is the one who enables us to live within this fellowship of self-giving love. He lives that we may live.

In John, Jesus spells out in remarkably clear and dramatic terms the nature of a God who lives to give himself away. This puts an interesting light on the subject of sacrifice. The human race universally seems to believe that sacrifice must be a part of the worship of deity. As a result, when anthropologists look for evidences of the religious dimension in any people's life, they look for traces of sacrifice. The assumption is that the gods demand, are assuaged by, or seek sacrifice from their worshipers. But Jesus pictures a new kind of deity: one who demands sacrifice from himself before sacrifice is accepted from his worshipers. The altar of all altars is not the one in the temple, but the one outside the Holy City on Golgotha—the cross—and the sacrifice on that altar is not a sheep or a human. The sacrifice is God himself in Christ.

This is a picture of the inner life of the triune Godhead—sacrificial self-giving. Jesus defines love by the sacrificial love of God, and he wants all who belong to him to experience it. Note his words to his own that Thursday night before the cross: "As the Father has loved me, so have I loved you.... My command is this: Love each other as I have loved you. Greater love has no one than this, that he lay down his life for his friends" (John 15:9, 12–13).

So the second person of the triune Godhead is free, but his freedom does not express itself in doing what he pleases for himself. It is freedom to do the will of his Father; in doing his Father's will, he finds his fulfillment. True freedom demands that he care more for another than for himself. Jesus gives us a new picture of God, but he is also giving us a picture of true personhood as it was meant to be, that is, truly free. And true freedom means free to give, not just to receive.

Created with a Moral Consciousness That Reflects the Holiness of God

If we are to take the persons of the Godhead as the patterns for our understanding of personhood, something must be said about holiness and moral consciousness, for from a biblical perspective holiness, love, and personhood must not be separated. The holy character of God who created us is reflected in the moral nature of the human person.

The essential nature of the God of Scripture is holy-love. All three persons of the Godhead are described as holy. Jesus, in the middle of his High Priestly Prayer in John 17, is praying for his disciples and cries out, "Holy Father, protect them by the power of your name–the name you gave me–so that they may be one as we are one" (John 17:11).

When no one else knew for sure who Jesus was, the devils Jesus exorcised did. At the beginning of his ministry, when Jesus is casting a demon from a demoniac in the synagogue in Capernaum, the demon cries out: "I know who you are–the Holy One of God!" (Mark 1:24). Simon Peter was in the synagogue that day and must never have forgotten it. Much later, when the demands of Jesus had been clarified and many who had believed in him had turned away, Jesus asked the Twelve if they were going to leave him too. Peter immediately responded: "Lord, to whom shall we go? You have the words of eternal life. We believe and know that you are the Holy One of God" (John 6:68–69). The Spirit seems to be almost synonymous with the concept of the holy in that the common appellation for him throughout Scripture is "Holy Spirit."

The New Testament builds on the Old Testament picture of Yahweh as the Holy One. Holiness is, as it were, his signature. Wherever one finds anything holy in the Old Testament, Yahweh is present, for he and he alone sanctifies. The day that belonged to him, the Sabbath, was to be a holy day. When God was in the burning bush, the ground surrounding it was holy. His people were to be holy because Yahweh, the Holy One who dwelt among them, was holy. The land to which Yahweh was taking his people was to be the "holy land," and the city in which he would dwell was to be called the "holy city." The temple where Yahweh met his people was "the holy place," and the room in which his presence resided was the "Holy of Holies" or "the most holy place." In the Levitical legislation, when Yahweh insisted that his people are to be different from the other peoples of the earth, he gave three simple reasons: "I am Yahweh," "I am holy," and "I am Yahweh who makes you holy" (Lev. 11:44–45; 19:3, 12, 14; 20:8). From Yahweh's point of view, the three statements are synonymous.

In his remarkable work *The Language and Imagery of the Bible*, G. B. Caird speaks about the use of figurative language in Scripture. He explains that we have no option but to use metaphor when we speak of God. The only language we have to describe the eternal God is our language–earthly, finite language of time and space. When Caird comes to the word *holy*, he knows he is dealing with a word that speaks of something from beyond our world. It is uniquely Yahweh's word, so Caird says: "All, or almost all, of the language used by the Bible to refer to God is metaphor (the one possible exception is the word *holy*)."[7]

When the angel Gabriel appeared to Mary to announce the coming conception of Jesus, he explained, "The *Holy Spirit* will come upon you, and the power of the Most High will overshadow you. So *the holy one* to be born will be called the Son of God" (Luke 1:35, emphasis added). God is holy, and the one who comes from him is holy.

So Jesus, the person who is the prototype for all human persons, the second person of the Holy Trinity, is holy. Does this mean that holiness is an essential part of all personhood? No, for if we say it is, then only three persons exist (the three in the divine Trinity), and the word *person* cannot be applied to any of us creatures who are made in God's image but have no inherent holiness. Perhaps a more accurate statement might be that the concept of personhood implies moral consciousness: the possibility to recognize moral choices and to respond to the call of a holy God. Persons have a potential for holiness. Any holiness we possess is a derived holiness. We have the possibility of becoming holy because of our relationship to that holy God.

To be human, to be a person, is to discern and to make moral judgments. A person cannot keep from being moral. A person may be immoral, but to be immoral is not to be amoral. Only the one with a moral capacity can be immoral. The world's most vehement moralizers often are the most immoral. When humans do wrong, they seem to have a compulsion to justify their evil on moral grounds. Persons cannot keep from making moral judgments about others, if not about themselves. To be a person is to have a sense of right and wrong, to know there is a difference between good and evil, justice and injustice. Unfortunately, there is in us no power adequate to realize in ourselves the standard that we unwittingly apply to others. In other words, as we have been saying all along, the source of the holy is never in us. Here is where we find a distinct difference between us and God. The power of the moral "ought" does not lie in the human "is." In God the "is" and the "ought" are the same.

This is what the philosophers are talking about when they say that in God "being" and "act" are one. Karl Barth spoke of God's being as his "Being-in-His-act" and his act as his "Act-in-his-Being."[8] Torrance develops this further: "In the Creator himself, Word, Person and Act are one and undivided, but in the creature this is not so…. Our speech and our action do not coincide in the unity and power of our person. Act and person, word and person, word and act, while not unrelated, are all separate. With God this is not the case, for his Word and his Act belong inseparably to the self-subsistence of his Person."[9]

In other words, when Paul says in Romans 7:15, "For what I want to do I do not do, but what I hate I do," he is speaking of an experience God has never had. In the Holy One, the "ought" and the "is" are not separated. With us it is different because the power of fulfillment for the ought is not in us, but such power does reside in the one from whom we have turned our faces. When the fellowship with God is broken, an internal contradiction begins to operate.

Not everyone agrees on the connecting of the moral with the holy as I have done here. Our Western understanding of the holy has been influenced too much by the Enlightenment and by the school of thought that produced Rudolf Otto and his influential work, *The Idea of the Holy.* For Otto, the moral and the holy were distinct and unrelated. The post-Enlightenment history of religion school greatly affected Otto's thinking. He came to the conclusion that the essence of the holy was simply that which was truly religious. Therefore, if he could identify the essence of the religious, he then would have identified the essence of the holy. So he began his search in the primitive religions of the world; for him, the religion of Israel was simply another religion. In fact, he found "the holy" in all religions. Therefore, if Israel had any distinctiveness in its faith and its God, for Otto the difference was one of degree, not one of ultimate nature, and could not be determinatively significant. Otto was not looking for the distinctions between religions. He was looking for what they all had in common.

What Otto found is summed up in his famous expression, "*mysterium tremendum et fascinans*" (tremendous and fascinating mystery). He was impressed by the concept of *mana*, an impersonal, supernatural force. Primitive peoples attribute to *mana* what in life is awesome, inexplicable, and ineluctable. Thus he spoke of the holy as the irrational "numinous." The holy for him had no element in it of either the rational or the ethical/moral. It was basically impersonal, and since ethics and morality are personal concepts that speak of interpersonal relations, the ethical/moral were not to be considered. The holy was that which in universal religion produced fear, awe, and wonder. In cases where the ethical and the moral were found in religion, they were imports, not necessarily native to religion.[10]

Many scholars are followers of Otto, unaware that they are illustrating the basic claim of Scripture about the holy: Yahweh, the Holy One of Israel, is the source of all holiness. He alone is holy in himself. Wherever we meet him, we find the holy present; contact with him always quickens moral consciousness. When Otto searched the religions of the world where Yahweh, the Holy One, could not be found, he found that humans can be religious without being moral or ethical. Therefore, the holy was impersonal and nonmoral. He found partial and perverted traces of humankind's original contact with the Holy One, traces left over after overt knowledge of the Holy One had been lost. He never found the holy itself. When Otto excluded Yahweh from his search, he precluded the possibility of finding what he sought.

A problem arises if we accept Otto's definition of *holy*. If we are made in the image of God, and if holiness is part of the prototype of our personhood, then it is clear that we are nonpersons or else something very significant to personhood is lacking in us. We must be badly damaged goods, persons with a moral ideal but without the power for its realization. If Adam and Eve were holy when they began their life together with God, they clearly did not continue long in that state. Genesis 3 tells of their separation from the presence of the Holy One. By Genesis 6:5, as God looked at his creation, he found that the thoughts and imaginations of human hearts were "only evil all the time." Any holiness they had known was now gone. They did not cease to be moral beings with ethical/moral consciousness. This is reflected first in their desire to hide from the face of Yahweh and, second, in the quickness with which they were willing to lay blame on each other.

The movement from good to evil is not a transition from the ethical/moral to the amoral but a transfer to the immoral, by definition a negative moral realm. By the time of the flood, people were still moral beings, each possessing an acute moral consciousness, especially as they related with other human beings. But their ethical/moral sensitivity was badly damaged. To be a person is to have an ethical/moral consciousness, even if it is twisted. Thus, we must add a fifth characteristic to human personhood: the fact of *ethical/moral consciousness and possibility*. To be a person is to be a maker of moral judgments, not just a maker of decisions.

This is a good place for a warning. When we think about the characteristics of personhood, it is important not to think of them as separable. They are interrelated in that they are simply different ways a person's functioning can be categorized. They are not different parts of a person. A person is an indivisible unit. These characteristics are not divisible adjuncts of one another. As persons

we are conscious that we are not alone;

we find ourselves in webs of relationships with others that are distinct from the self;

our relationships are not one-way, because the person is acted upon as well as being an initiator of action;

the most personal of those actions are not determined by any force external to the person;

each person could have done otherwise in these most personal relations;

relations can be both constructive and destructive;

each person is responsible for the consequences of his or her action.

In other words, we know that we are selves who are planted in reciprocal webs of relationships and who are free and moral by definition.

At the human level we see evidences of personal freedom in the sense of violation that comes to us when another's will has been forced upon us or when we have been used for another's self-interests. Persons intuitively know they should be respected and should never be treated as objects to be used or violated. They are not to be controlled but solicited. These characteristics of human persons are what ultimately force the collapse of all political totalitarianisms. Persons are not the property of any institution, and any structure that assumes that they are is in conflict with a reality that will ultimately undo it. Persons are to be determined from within, not from without; and the inner determination is to be by free choice, not by instinct or external constraint.

This is why God can be called holy. Holiness is a moral and ethical category and is possible only where there is freedom. God is explicably free. His holiness is expressed in his freedom. He chooses truth and self-sacrificing love, which seek the well-being of every other person. The inner *perichoretic* relation of the three persons of the Trinity is holy-love, and its glory is that it is the free expression of the divine choice of Father, Son, and Holy Spirit.

Here we note a major distinction between animals and humans. Animals are not made in the image of God. They are not persons and do not know the openness of choice that characterizes personhood. Impersonal and ineluctable forces–instincts–control animals. That is why we do not characterize the actions of animals or natural forces as moral. Only persons are moral beings and have the freedom to make moral choices. This freedom makes righteousness possible but at the same time enables humans to sin. We do not speak of the destructive force of an earthquake or a tornado as evil. We do speak of genocide or rape as evil. These are the acts of persons who are capable of choice. Nature knows no such freedom. As there can be no evil without freedom, neither can there be any holiness.

The basis for human freedom is found in the fact that God made us in his own image as persons and moral creatures. That is why we can love. We cannot love unless we are free. Note the contrast between lust and love: the person controlled by lust is willing to use another for his or her ends, to violate the other person's freedom. A person who truly loves will not. Persons are made for love, and it is in the freedom of love that persons find their fulfillment. We are made in the image of the Son, not in necessity, but in freedom.

The law of God is posited on this freedom. The law given at Sinai is apodictic in character, but it assumes that those who are bound by it are bound by choice. God seeks a people who will love him with all of their hearts and minds. External obedience is never enough to please him. What he wants is a personal relationship of loving trust given by a creature who freely chooses the relationship. God can make such forces of nature as wind and sea obey him, but those forces cannot return to him the faithful love he seeks. They are not persons. Thus, the new covenant law is written on the hearts of God's people, and they respond to him in love. God will give his Spirit to his people if they will receive him, and the Spirit will place the free love of God within the inner life of God's people. Thus, the law is not supposed to be an external factor of power, but a compliment and a complement to human capacity. When accompanied by the Spirit, the law is actually a promise that fits the human person's potential in the Spirit.

Created to Live in Openness

Openness, the next characteristic of personhood – seen so clearly in Jesus, has two particular aspects. The first is *self-transcendence*, although it has a variety of names. John Zizioulas speaks of "ecstasy"[11] and Robert Jenson of "self-transcendence."[12] E. L. Mascall, in his Gifford Lectures, referred to the "openness of being."[13] What these and others are trying to describe is the fact that the true person is characterized by an other-orientedness within the self that enables one to see oneself as others see him; to separate oneself as it were from oneself; to stand outside oneself; and to evaluate oneself and one's world morally and cognitively. That is why Zizioulas speaks of "ecstasy," the root meaning of which is "to stand outside oneself."

The poignant illustration of self-transcendence lies in the conscience, the human ability to look at and critique oneself. Persons are moral beings and as such hold themselves to a moral standard. Something within a person second-guesses the person and ethically and morally criticizes the self. One might think there were two selves within, one of which feels responsible for keeping the other straight. Every person has his or her own accuser within. That is the key factor in human accountability. To crush that inner voice is to dehumanize oneself. We cannot impose our way upon the world without doing damage to ourselves and to other people.

Therefore, human cognition falls under this category of self-transcendence because the ability to reason elevates a human person above all the rest of creation. Pascal speaks of this in *Penseés* when he identifies man as "a thinking reed."[14] He defines thinking as an inner dialogue, an inner conversation. His observation is confirmed in the fact that it is normal for languages to have both independent personal pronouns and reflexive personal pronouns. The rustic who said, "I sez to myself, sez I," undoubtedly knew little of philosophy, grammar, or psychology and was nonplussed by his neighbor's response: "Now who's talking to whom?" Within the human person there is an otherness that insists on separating from the self in order to assist the self in its pursuit of truth and reality. The reflexive pronouns are the necessary result. We need them to deal with and express our realities. The personal subject can become its own object. The subject/object relationship becomes a description of an inner relationship within the self as well as a relationship of the self to its external world. Persons have a remarkable capacity to look at themselves. It is as if the inner person knows that it must not lose itself in itself and must reach beyond the self.

The second aspect of openness is *permeability*. The power of self-transcendence, the ability to stand outside of oneself, carries with it a certain permeability. Each person has an inner necessity to relate to the world beyond the self. Something within the human spirit is unwilling to let the self be the final arbiter in all matters. The cry of the conscience is an appeal to an objective moral reality extrinsic to the person but having its echoes at the deepest inner level of the person.

This explains the universality of the experience of guilt. To be a person is to have that capacity. Cognitive activity within a person is also an implicit acknowledgment of a world beyond the person, which the person needs to know realistically. There is no room for solipsism here. The person cannot escape the world around and beyond. He or she must relate to it in one way or another.

Jesus was acutely aware of his world with its multiple elements. He knew what it included: the Father and the Spirit, Satan, angels, Caiaphas and Herod, the poor, the sick, the demonized, the multitudes, and his own family and friends. There was an order in his relationship to all of these. There was a chosen center that, when in place, determined all other relationships. That center was the Father who had sent him and whose will he had chosen to make his own. There was *openness* in his personhood to a beyond, to other persons–the Father and the Spirit–in whom he found for himself the reason for all things. The key to understanding Jesus did not lie in Jesus. It lay beyond him. He lived joyously from Another, through Another, and for Another. Jesus was the divine Son of God and a perfect human being, yet he did not find himself complete within himself. He was not the center of his own chosen existence.

Once again we note how biblical thought often is in direct contradiction to much of modern thought about the self. Taking note of the triumph in psychology of what Robert Bellah calls the "therapeutic self," Stanley Grenz comments:

> The triumph of the therapeutic that accompanies the culture of self-fulfillment enthrones the self as monarch. In this emergent kingdom of the self, the individual self is looked to as providing the "center" that is able to hold together even as the surrounding world disintegrates. Moreover, the individual self assumes the role of being arbiter and focal point of meaning, values, and even existence itself. Hence, Allport defines values psychologically as "simply *meanings perceived as related to self.*" And the highest value that this self can posit is freedom,

which when understood as the flip side of self-consciousness or self-awareness, involves the capacity either to mold or to actualize oneself. The elevation of the self to the center of the world leads likewise to a corresponding transformation of the concept of health. Health, understood in the sense of personal well-being (i.e., the well-being of the self), no longer remains either the means to some higher end or the by-product of commitment to some great good but emerges as the goal of living itself.[15]

Clearly, the modern social sciences have little grasp of what it means to be a person in the manner in which we have acknowledged that personhood's original meaning is relationship and mutuality. Science's concept of the self and Jesus' understanding of what it means to be a person are polar opposites.

Since Jesus is the original pattern – the prototype, for the human person – who demonstrates what a normal and perfect person is, it is safe to say that to be a person, even a perfect person, is to be *incomplete*, that no person is ever complete in himself or herself. The person's completeness lies in an other. The Son is not complete in himself. He draws life from the Father and lives life to please his Father. The Father must define fatherhood in terms of the Son. His completion as Father lies in the Son and in the Spirit through whom he does his work. The Spirit is the Spirit of the Father and the Son. He does not speak from himself. He speaks that which he receives from the Father and the Son. He does not claim to be Truth as Jesus does. Jesus says that the Spirit will lead the disciples into the truth, which means that he, the Spirit, will lead them to the Son. The Spirit does not speak of himself. He glorifies the Son and takes what is the Son's and makes it known to the disciples of Jesus. Not one of the persons of the Trinity is complete in himself even though divine.

If incompleteness is true of divine persons, how much more true it must be of created persons. There is completeness in the oneness of the being of God that has no correspondence within the human being, who is a finite, created creature. The divine being in the rich interpersonal life of the triune Godhead is completely self-subsistent and needs nothing beyond itself. God as God exists in himself. He has, as the scholars say, aseity.

Individual human beings know nothing comparable to that. As creatures, our existence is a gift from beyond that we neither merit nor can sustain but perpetually must receive. We subsist at the gracious mercy of life's Giver. Our incompleteness is in our own being as well as in our personhood. Our personhood reflects the *imago Dei* more than our individuality. We are not self-subsistent beings. And that personhood, like the Person of which it is an image, cries for another. Like the eternal Son, we find our completeness in relation to our Source and our Sustainer. The person who is alone is not a whole person, because no person is ever supposed to be completely alone. That would be to have entered into hell.

Created to Relate to Others in Trusting Love

Since personhood by definition is marked by an openness that reaches beyond itself, and a person is thereby incomplete in himself or herself, a person finds completeness only in *being related to others in trusting love*. Here again our original, the triune God, defines us. The persons of the Godhead are self-consciously individual in their personhood. The Son is not the Father or the Spirit, and he senses his difference from both. The Father is not the Son or the Spirit, and he knows himself to be distinct from both. Likewise the Spirit is the Spirit of the Father and of the Son, but he is neither the Father nor the Son. Yet, even though each is distinct, he cannot be found in separation from the other two persons. (The only exception to this is in the dereliction of Christ on the cross.) They only are found in their distinctiveness *in* each other. The completeness of each person of the triune Godhead is found in identification with the other two. They are personally three, although ontologically they are one, and the personal distinctions are necessary for God to be love. Since to love is to give oneself, one cannot love if he has nothing to give and no one to give it to. So God is the original of all things, a communion of three distinct persons whose existence consists in the giving and receiving of themselves to and from each other. Self-giving constitutes their being.

Jesus explains that he can do nothing of himself; that his life is not his own; that he draws life from the Father through the Spirit; that his desire is not to do his own will but that of the Father. His relationship of trusting love with the Father is assumed when Jesus talks about losing one's life to find it. In all three Synoptic Gospels, when Jesus first begins to speak to his disciples about the cross, he insists that to find true life one must lose oneself in a cause other than one's own (Matt. 16:25; Mark 8:35; Luke 9:24). Self-protection, the refusal to give away oneself, he says, is self-loss and death.

Self-loss is what is on Jesus' mind during that last week before the cross when some Greeks wanted to see him. His response, as he faces the cross, is that the one who *loves* his own life will lose it, and that the one who *hates* his own life will find it. In order to live, he says, a grain of wheat must fall into the ground and die. Too often these comments have been interpreted as applicable only to human beings, to *sinful* human beings, but Jesus applies them to himself, the Sinless One. He does not seem to be speaking from his human nature alone. If the eternal Son of God protected himself, refused to trust himself to the will of his Father, and ceased to live for someone other than himself, he would cease to be who he is, because God by definition is self-giving love. A person as a person, human or divine, finds fullness of life only in one beyond oneself. Christ came, died, and was raised again to make possible the reestablishment of fullness of personhood in people like you and me.

Paul seems to have understood the necessity of being related in trusting love. How else do we explain his obsession with the cross and his conviction that he, along with everyone else who believes, should be participants in it? This is why Paul can say he is crucified with Christ but this crucifixion does not end in death. Its result is new life, which is really Christ's life lived within him. On the Damascus Road, at the end of Paul's (Saul's) self-contained, self-directed life, he finds, not death, but freedom and fullness of real life, life lived as a person is supposed to live.

After all, the Christian life begins with the symbol of baptism. Baptism not only signifies death to the old life with its sin; it also symbolizes death to the *source* of the old life, which is the self. Baptism signifies the beginning of a new life lived out of another source, Christ and his Spirit. The Spirit, who raised Jesus from the dead, is the one who enables new life in us. That Spirit wants to raise us from the death of living in and out of ourselves. We receive the Spirit when we believe; the Spirit begets the very life of Christ within us. Thus, Paul can tell the Colossians, "Christ ... is your life" (3:4). They should actually imitate God and live in the agape love that cares more for another than for itself, the love that Christ manifested when he gave himself for us.

The radical nature of this new life that the Spirit brings is reviewed in Ephesians 5:1 where Paul tells us to "imitate" God. What mortal could ever be like God? How to do that, of course, depends on what one thinks God is like. If one thinks of power and omniscience as the supreme attributes of God, then Paul's instructions are absurd. Or if one thinks of God in his perfection of moral rectitude, what mortal could boast of that? But if the essence of the divine nature is self-sacrificing love, it is possible for us to imitate God. "Be imitators of God, therefore, as dearly loved children and live a life of love, just as Christ loved us and gave himself up for us as a fragrant offering and sacrifice to God" (Eph. 5:1–2).

Self-giving love is "fragrant." If we think such a life is an unattainable ideal, how can we explain Paul's claim that Timothy lived in self-giving love (Phil. 2:19–21)? Apparently Paul thinks that all Christians can and should live as those who seek, not their own good, but the things that are of Christ Jesus. Note his word to the Corinthians: "Let no one seek the things of himself but the things that pertain to others" (1 Cor. 10:24, literal translation). Note also his surprising personal confession: "I try to please everybody in every way. For I am not seeking *my own good* [literally "the things of myself"] but the good of many, so that they may be saved. Follow my example, as I follow the example of Christ" (1 Cor. 10:33–11:1, emphasis added).[16] Paul is not wallowing in self-pity. Rather, he is exulting in the joy of the fullness of personhood available in Christ, a personhood expressed in self-giving, trusting love.

The idea of living continually in self-giving love is a bit shocking to most modern and postmodern Christians. Yet the divine reality of our lives is built around the idea that I find myself and my fulfillment in others. To recapitulate our discussion thus far:

> No *human person is self-originating.* The choice to bring each of us into existence was made by two other people, so our life is a gift from others. We begin our life in another.

> No *human person is ever self-sustaining.* We live by that which is not from within us. First, we draw our life from our mother; then we live from our mother's milk; we ultimately live from the bounty of nature, whose elements and richness we take into ourselves, including food, water, oxygen, friendship, encouragement, and inspiration.

> No *person is self-explanatory.* There is no such thing as a typical human being. We come in two editions, and two who are different from each other are needed to explain any one of us. The male finds his definition in relation to the female, just as the female finds her identity in terms of differentiation from her sexual opposite. Our biology insists that our completion is in another. Each of us is made for another who is distinct and different.

If we as persons, then, are not self-originating, self-sustaining, or self-explanatory, why should it come as a shock to us that we are not self-fulfilling, that we are by definition made for a love that *gives* itself in trust. Tom Torrance speaks of the divine existence as "the Being of God for others."[17] The author of the book of Hebrews speaks of Christ's sacrifice as an occasion of joy. Even the Christ found his fulfillment outside of himself. The whole biblical story, as well as all human existence, is support for the idea that we were made to give ourselves to one another in other-oriented love.

HUMAN PERSONHOOD ENABLES IDENTIFICATION BETWEEN GOD AND HIS CREATURES

Adam and Eve were made in the divine image. The likeness between the Creator and creature is close enough that the two, God and his humans, can commune with each other and know each other as persons.

In Genesis the Edenic garden scene pictures the communion between God and Adam and Eve–the climax of the creation story. We find later in Genesis that the highest divine compliment is the privilege of walking with God. Such communion between creature and Creator is not just an ideal to be dreamed about, but God's intended purpose for humanity. In fact, that communion can be described as life and salvation.

Jesus explains in John 10 that his purpose in coming to the world is that he, the Good Shepherd, might give abundant life to his sheep. In his High Priestly Prayer he explains, "This is eternal life: that they may know you, the only true God, and Jesus Christ, whom you have sent" (John 17:3). The night before the cross, Jesus makes his intention known for all of his disciples: he wants them to be where he is. Implicit within the decision that we should be made in God's very image was the intention that we should be capable of communion with God. He made us so that we can know him and walk with him. This knowledge is reciprocal–God knowing humanity and humans knowing God.

It is impossible to know another who is closed to you. Paul confirms this notion in his letter to the Galatian believers; he was the one who had brought the knowledge of God to them. He says, "Formerly ... you did not know God.... But now that you know God ..." (4:8–9). Then he corrects himself: "or rather are known by God." Here we see that the knowledge God seeks is not subject/object knowledge but subject/subject, I-Thou, knowledge between persons.[18] God covets not simply rational knowledge *about* another, but actually personally *knowing* another, the kind of knowledge that Paul suggests even the all-knowing God cannot have with us without our consent.

The knowledge of God that leads to salvation is very personal. We see this truth spelled out in John 14–17 in the conversations Jesus had with his disciples and with his Father immediately before his arrest and trial. The desire for personal knowledge is expressed in his use of the figure of the vine with its branches and in his use of the preposition *in*. In John 15:1–8 Jesus develops the metaphor of the vine, in which the Father is the gardener, Jesus is the "true vine," and the disciples are the branches. He explains that the branches draw their life from the vine, and that apart from the vine they can do nothing. The fruitfulness of the branches depends on an unbroken connection between the branches and the vine. The branch must abide *in* the vine so that the life of the vine can be in the branch. Likewise, the fruitfulness of the disciples will come simply from their abiding *in* him so that the life that is *in* him can exist *in* them. The relationship of abiding is to be like Christ's relationship of abiding *in* the Father.

Philip asked for the privilege of seeing the Father (John 14:8). Jesus insisted that anyone who had seen him had seen the Father. Then he asked the eleven remaining disciples: "Don't you believe that I am *in* the Father, and that the Father is *in* me? The words I say to you are not just my own. Rather, it is the Father living *in* me, who is doing his work. Believe me when I say that I am *in* the Father and the Father is *in* me" (vv. 10–11, emphasis added). Jesus draws his life from the Father and can do nothing from himself. Even the words he speaks are not his alone. All he does emerges from his relationship with the Father. He abides in the Father as the branch abides in the vine, and the life that results in him flows from the Father through him to the world. That is the kind of relationship the disciples are to have with him.

An understanding of this metaphor about the vine does not just depend on one's knowledge of horticulture. To know what Jesus is speaking about, one must have an understanding of *perichoresis*, how the Father and the Son live in each other. Perhaps, since the vine and its branches are the work of the Creator himself, the concept of *perichoresis* can help us understand a bit better the life of the vine.

Jesus underscores his concern for his disciples in the conclusion of his prayer to his Father (John 17:20–23). Jesus tells the Father that he is not praying simply for his eleven disciples, but for all who will believe on him in the future. The intimate relationship he is describing, which exists between him and his Father, is God's will not only for the original disciples, but also for every person who will ever believe. He prays that Christian believers will know oneness with God like the personal oneness the Son and the Father have. His prayer to the Father is that all believers may be *in* the Father and *in* the Son just as the Father is *in* the Son and the Son is *in* the Father. His purpose: "May they also be *in* us so that the world may believe that you have sent me" (v. 21, emphasis added). He concludes, "I have given them the glory that you gave me, that they may be one as we are one: I *in* them and you *in* me" (vv. 22–23, emphasis added).

The relationship of which he is speaking is much deeper than simply an experience of forensic justification or the pardoning of our sins. It is much more than a change in legal status before God. There is to be such a commonality between the life of the believer and that of the three persons of the triune Godhead that the world, in seeing the way the believer lives, can believe that Jesus is the Son whom the Father has sent into the world, the very incarnate reflection of the God who reigns over all. Undoubtedly this kind of relationship is in Paul's mind when he says, "For to me, to live is Christ" (Phil. 1:21) and "Christ lives in me" (Gal. 2:20). Christ is Paul's very life, so that Paul's life can become the very life of Christ for others! Paul says to the Corinthians:

> But thanks be to God, who always leads us in triumphal procession *in* Christ and through us spreads everywhere the fragrance of the knowledge of him. For we are to God the aroma of Christ among those who are being saved and those who are perishing. To the one we are the smell of death; to the other, the fragrance of life. (2 Cor. 2:14–16, emphasis added)

We are to live in God. Because he is love, we are to live in love even as the persons of the triune Godhead live in love.

All of what I am saying here assumes a biblical view of personhood, personhood as we see it in Jesus Christ. Everyday life is a symbol pointing to the way that life is intended to work. Since we seldom look for the witness that life itself brings to the Father, Son, and Spirit, we often miss seeing the data before us. The paradigm with which we approach the Scriptures and life is too narrow. An inadequate concept of personhood will not give us the categories to identify what we all have experienced.

Karol Wojtyla has put us in his debt with his play *The Jeweler's Shop.* The story takes place in three acts, and each act is the story of a couple. The first act is the account of a young couple who fall in love and marry. The wife becomes pregnant; the husband goes off to war and is killed. So the son who is born never sees his father, and the father, of course, never sees the son. The second act is the story of another couple. They marry, have three children, and slowly drift apart. The second couple is in striking contrast to the couple in the first act. They live under the same roof, eat at the same table, sleep in the same bed, but they exist in totally separate worlds. The third act is the story of the son of the first couple and the daughter of the second couple. They fall in love and try to establish the relational basis for a successful marriage. One scene in the second act dramatically portrays the human counterpart of the divine *perichoresis*, albeit negatively.

Anna, the wife in the second scene, is reflecting on the rift that has developed between her and her husband, Stefan. She says:

> *I could not reconcile myself to this,*
> *nor could I prevent*
> *a rift opening between us*
> *(its edges stood still at first,*
> *but at any moment they could move apart*
> *wider and wider –*
> *at any rate, I did not feel them*
> *moving closer together again).*
>
> *It was as if Stefan had ceased to be in me.*
> *Did I cease to be in him too?*
> *Or was it simply that I felt*
> *I now existed only in myself?*
> *At first I felt such a stranger*
> *in myself!*
> *It was as if I had become unaccustomed to the walls of*
> *my interior –*
> *so full had they been of Stefan*
> *that without him they seemed empty.*
> *Is it not too terrible a thing*
> *to have committed the walls of my interior*
> *to a single inhabitant*
> *who could disinherit my self*

and somehow deprive me of my place in it?
Outwardly nothing changed.
Stefan seemed to behave the same,
but he could not heal the wound
that had opened in my soul.[19]

Human persons were made for each other. Our fulfillment in life depends on other people; this need for another is a reflection of the triune God who lives in a community of three persons. What Wojtyla is doing in this play is informing us that the world shows more signs than we realize of being the creation of a God who is in himself *perichoretic* life and love.

But without a biblical understanding of personhood, we do not have the categories to recognize the evidence when it is all around us. Once we see what the prototype is like, we recognize the traces of the image in ourselves and understand better both the suffering and the joys inherent in being human.

Four

THE HUMAN PROBLEM

WHY IS IDENTIFICATION WITH GOD IMPOSSIBLE?

The discussion in the preceding chapters brings us now to the problem of all problems.

A BIBLICAL UNDERSTANDING OF SIN

God is holy-love and has made his human creatures in his own image as persons. They are made for intimate communion with the one who is holy-love. In fact, they are made for love—self-giving holy-love.

One would think, on the basis of what I have said so far, that the story of human history should be a delightful account of the true, the good, the beautiful, and the holy. Our world was made and is sustained by this God. He is sovereign and reigns without rival or competitor. He is God and God alone. The question then is why the world and its history are not more marked by the divine character than they are. History does have its saints, but why are they the exceptions? Persons are made for love, but that very capacity is part of a moral character that gives them the power to sin. And humanity has sinned! In fact, *sin* is more descriptive of God's human world than is *holiness*, although we all are the work of his holy hands. Indeed, we sinned early!

Before the third chapter of Genesis is completed, the original couple, made for each other and for fellowship with God who is love, are alienated from God. They are distrustful of him and each other, resentful of each other, and banished from Paradise. They are living in a cursed world, one in which life's sweetest fulfillments are touched by suspicion, pain, frustration, and bitterness under the ever-threatening shadow of death. The natural good–the pattern for life–now seems unattainable, and the evil–which does not even belong–reigns. The spouses, who were made to find their fulfillment in self-giving love to each other and to the God who gave them life, now use each other for selfish ends and blame each other for the unpleasant consequences that they experience from their own individual choices. Polygamy replaces monogamy, and woman, made to be man's valued partner, becomes his possession for personal exploitation, to be used instead of gloried in and lived for. Fraternal relations are no better. Brother kills brother, and the thoughts and imaginations of human hearts are "evil all the time" (Gen. 6:5). The human has become inhumane. The glory is gone.

Even the natural world seems to be at odds with itself. What was Paradise now is wilderness, and the fruitful garden is a jungle in which no one is safe. Sodom and Gomorrah are the logical consequence. God looks at his creation and grieves. His heart is filled with pain as he views his handiwork. The rest of the Scripture from the end of Genesis 3 to the conclusion of the book of Revelation presents a consistent picture of tragedy. The most sacred things have lost their original glory, and those beings who were from the beginning good in themselves are now the perpetrators of evil. A world that God originally said was "good, very good" has changed.

Isaiah and Ezekiel describe the Holy City, Jerusalem, God's own city, in just such tragic terms. Israel's capital city, the site of the temple, the dwelling place of God, was the center of monotheistic worship in the world. The city was heir to the moral and ethical revelations of Sinai. Yet now God finds his own city unfit to be his dwelling.

The picture Isaiah presents fits the picture given in Genesis 6, not that of Genesis 2. The hands of the citizens are stained with blood (59:3), their tongues speak lies, their hands are filled with violence, and their deeds are evil. Justice has fallen in the streets, and no one cries out for the vanquished innocents that suffer. It is a city of moral darkness where one stumbles at midday "as if it were twilight" (v. 10). Those compelled to move in such blackness grope for a wall to guide them through the moral murk as they stumble to find their way. One needs to "light the lanterns at noon." Ruin and destruction are the marks of the city's life because of Israel's "rebellion and treachery against the LORD" (v. 13). God sees the city in its need and looks for a single person to care, with whom God can begin to reverse the evil. He cannot find one. Even the All-knowing One is astounded at the total, all-encompassing character of the evil of the city, his Holy City.

Ezekiel, at the end of the seventh and the beginning of the sixth century BC, gives us a very similar picture of the Holy City in chapter 22. The princes are using their positions and their powers to oppress and mistreat the powerless, the stranger, the orphans, and the widows. They worship pagan deities and ravage the women of the city. Sexual aberrations of every sort leave no human relations sacrosanct. Bribery and extortion are the order, and murder is unexceptional. The princes are like roaring lions preying upon those whose well-being is their responsibility. The priests do violence to the very law they teach. They profane the holy things they are ordained to protect. They are unable to make a distinction between the sacred and the profane, between the clean and the unclean. These who are ordained to serve the Holy One give themselves to the profanation of the sacred, and sacrilege becomes an art. Jerusalem's prophets are no better than the princes and the priests. Those who are to be the bearers of the divine word offer lying divinations and false visions as sacred truth to those who come to them. They say, "God has spoken," when the Lord in his displeasure has become silent. The Lord, in his desire not to destroy the city he loves and which bears his name, again seeks a single person who sees, who cares, and who will intercede (v. 30). He cannot find *one*.

Likewise, God tells Jeremiah: "Go up and down the streets of Jerusalem, look around and consider, search through her squares. If you can find but one person who deals honestly and seeks the truth, I will forgive this city" (Jer. 5:1). But not one is to be found.

The picture we find in the New Testament is no different. In Romans 1 Paul speaks of his own world; it is one of godlessness and wickedness where people suppress the truth. Those who know God do not glorify him and have no gratitude. They become so futile in their thinking that birds, animals, and reptiles replace the Holy One–the Lord God, their Creator and Redeemer–as objects of worship. Lust replaces love and reigns unabated. The unnatural takes the place of the natural, the indecent the place of the decent, and the perverse the place of the appropriate. Envy, greed, strife, deceit, slander, insolence, and ruthlessness are the norm. Paul concludes that all have sinned and fallen short of God's intent and purposes. There is no exception. He turns to the Scriptures to support his analysis in Romans 3:10–18:

> *There is no one righteous, not even one;*
>   *there is no one who understands,*
>   *no one who seeks God.*
> *All have turned away,*
>   *they have together become worthless;*
> *there is no one who does good,*
>   *not even one. (cf. Ps. 14:1–3)*
>
> *Their throats are open graves;*
>   *their tongues practice deceit. (cf. Ps. 5:9)*
>
> *The poison of vipers is on their lips. (cf. Ps. 140:3)*
>
> *Their mouths are full of cursing and bitterness. (cf. Ps. 10:7)*
>
> *Their feet are swift to shed blood;*
>   *ruin and misery mark their ways,*
>   *and the way of peace they do not know. (cf. Isa. 59:7–8)*
> *There is no fear of God before their eyes. (cf. Ps. 36:1)*

The picture presented in Romans 3 is not pretty. The world is now a far cry from Eden with its loving, open, face-to-face communion between God and his creatures. The world is under a curse, and even nature shares in the tragedy that marks the life of humankind. The whole creation, human and otherwise, groans for redemption (Rom.

8:19-22). How could a world so good–God's world–fall so far? The picture in Romans fits that of Isaiah, Jeremiah, and Ezekiel. God looked for a second Adam with whom he could begin again and create a new world, but there was no one. The problem in God's creation had to be solved where it was. The problem was not in heaven; nor was it in God. The problem was in us, God's creatures, and must be solved there. Thus, the incarnation was necessary. When there was no such human person among us, God had to become one. So Jesus Christ was born.

Occasionally there are some who will suggest that the biblical picture is entirely too pessimistic, that humankind's problem is not so deep, that sometime somewhere humanity will be able to cure its existential sickness and produce a world in which righteousness and justice can prevail. The close of the nineteenth century was marked by just such optimism. The period was characterized by sentimental liberalism that saw the world on an evolutionary lift, being carried onward and inexorably upward. Thus, liberal Christianity envisioned the coming twentieth century as the "the Christian century." Yet all of us now know that the twentieth century was the most universally violent century in human history. The beginning of the twenty-first century seems to promise more of the same. At no time has the biblical picture seemed more realistic. It describes our world as one that is fallen and in need of a savior.

We Turned Our Faces Away from Him

What went wrong? The answer of the Scripture to that question is intriguingly simple. Multiple expressions describe the cause behind this tragic story, but all point to one simple fact: a separation produced by sin had come between the creature and his God (Isa. 59:2). A chasm had opened up between humankind and their Maker. God's face could no longer be seen. The divine presence was no longer a welcomed part of human life. The tie to the source of all truth and virtue, the one who is holy-love and holy-love's only source, was broken. But what caused the break?

The New Testament blames it all on Adam. Note the words of Paul: "Just as sin entered the world through one man, and death through sin, and in this way death came to all men, because all sinned.... The result of one trespass was condemnation for all men" (Rom. 5:12, 18).

But what was the nature of Adam's sin, and why and how did it produce such doleful results that affected all of humankind? His sin was not the violation of a moral code like that later given to Israel at the exodus. Paul's paradigm is not that of Sinai but Eden. Sinai's law was not yet known. That came later when God was dealing with a nation in a fallen world. Adam's misstep was something infinitely simpler. It was a change in the personal relationship of the creature to his Maker and Lord that made it necessary for Yahweh later to spell out the law. Adam and Eve together chose a relationship of personal distrust, distance, suspicion, and disobedience rather than one of open and loving trust, friendship, and obedience. And behind the shift from trust and communion to suspicion and separation was an overriding concern for themselves.

These two were the crowning glory of the creation, made in the very image and likeness of God. To them God had lovingly given individual existence, each other, a universe to enjoy, and incomparable communion. But their choice changed their relationship from God-centered, other-oriented, and reciprocal affection to individual and self-centered behavior. Luther used a phrase that graphically depicts what happened. He spoke of "a heart curved in on itself" (*cor incurvatus ad se*). Hearts made for other-oriented holy-love, hearts that before their sin were centered in God as their Friend, instead turned inward and centered in themselves. Adam and Eve chose to act as lords in the kingdom of him who is Lord of all.

In his picture of the suffering servant, Isaiah says:

> *We all, like sheep, have gone astray,*
>   *each of us has turned to his own way;*
> *and the* LORD *has laid on him*
>   *the iniquity of us all.* (53:6, *emphasis added*)

We all have strayed, but not like the innocent wandering of sheep. The Hebrew word *panah*, translated here as "turned," is actually the root from which comes the Hebrew word for "face" (*panim*). A literal translation of the verse could be, "We have *faced* every one to his own way." We shifted our attention from the source of all good and turned in an act of rejection and rebellion to our own individual interests.

So the sin that started the problem was a deliberate reorientation, a turning of our faces away from our Friend and Source to "our own way." A shift in the center of gravity for the human psyche was made by a deliberate act. Man and woman chose to center themselves in themselves, to make self the point of reference. The Holy One–who is other-oriented love, who gave them life, who sustained that life, and who was their true fulfillment–was now rejected. To use Paul Tillich's phrase, Adam and Eve became their own "ultimate concern." The place of God in human persons' lives had been taken by those persons themselves. Despite the fact that God is by definition the center of creation, the creature had decided to make itself the center of its own individual existence. God's creature assumed the position that belonged to God alone.

Emil Brunner speaks rightly of this as a perversion of the relationship that had existed between man and God.

> Existence is now turned in the opposite direction. God has been removed from the centre, and we are in the centre of the picture; our life has become ec-centric. The lie that we are the centre is characteristic of our present life. We "revolve around ourselves." The dominant note in our life is no longer the *dominus* but the rebel: the "I" itself. *Cor incurvatum in se*, the self which is bent back upon itself.... In every chorus of this life, the self which seeks itself is the leader of the chorus. The broken relationship with God means the perversion and poisoning of all the functions of life.... By sin, the nature of man, not merely something in his nature, is changed and perverted.[1]

Since God is the center of all things, Brunner sees humankind centering in himself as the supreme example of pride, an actual self-deification in which humanity tries to fulfill Satan's promise to Adam and Eve: "You will be like God" (Gen. 3:5).

The whole world is yours, but its centre is not yours. Its centre is God Himself. To infringe His sovereign rights, His divine privilege, is to desire to be like God. What happens then, if you still insist on doing it? The Lord says, 'Thou shalt surely die'; the serpent says, 'Ye shall be as God.' The story of autonomous humanity may well show us which was speaking the truth.[2]

Isaiah gives us a graphic picture of Babylon's (Lucifer's) arrogance.

You said in your heart,
  "I will ascend to heaven;
I will raise my throne
    above the stars of God;
I will sit enthroned on the mount of assembly,
    on the utmost heights of the sacred mountain.
I will ascend above the tops of the clouds;
    I will make myself like the Most High."
    (14:13-14, emphasis added)

God continues his description of Babylon, the symbol of human sin.

Now then, listen, you wanton creature,
    lounging in your security
and saying to yourself,
    "I am, and there is none besides me.
I will never be a widow
    or suffer the loss of children."...
You have trusted in your wickedness
    and have said, "No one sees me."
Your wisdom and knowledge mislead you
    when you say to yourself,
"I am, and there is none besides me." (Isa. 47:8, 10, emphasis added)

Sin characterizes the person whose starting point of reference always is the self, the person in whom the "I" has taken the place of God. The Hebrew is more poignant in the above passage than the English; in the two cases in which the English translation has the symbol of sin saying

"I am" (vv. 8, 10), the Hebrew simply has the first personal pronoun "I" (*ani*): "and saying to yourself, 'I,' and there is none besides," and "When you say to yourself, 'I,' and there is none besides me." The one who knows these passages immediately recognizes the expression, "and there is none besides," as one of the most distinctive descriptions that Yahweh, the God of Israel, claims for himself in Isaiah. The speaker is thinking and speaking words that only God can utter. So sin occurs when the human person takes God's place in his or her own life. Adam and Eve turned away from their Source. They centered their existence in themselves. The problem arose when they turned toward the self.

The Hebrew of the Old Testament gives further evidence to help us. Three words in particular are used in the Hebrew Scriptures to describe this turning. This is not the place for an exhaustive study of this vocabulary. It is helpful, however, to realize how simple and clear these words are. The first is the Hebrew word to which we have already referred, *panah*, from which the word for *face* comes. So to sin is to turn one's face away from God. This is consonant with the phrase translated "disobey" (*lo' shema' leqol*), but which literally means "not to hearken to the voice of" or "not to give attention to." These words connote not just a relationship to an objective legal code, but a relationship with another person from whom we have turned and now are ignoring.

The second and third words for "turn" are *sur* and *shuv(b)*. Both are spatial, positional, and directional terms. They are used of a change in direction of face, body, steps, or attention. A typical use of the first of these (*sur*) is found in Exodus where God speaks of Israel's apostasy in the case of the golden calf: "They have been quick to *turn* away (*sur*) from what I commanded them and have made themselves an idol cast in the shape of a calf. They have bowed down to it and sacrificed to it and said, 'These are your gods, O Israel, who brought you up out of Egypt'" (32:8, emphasis added). Numerous other instances could be cited of the use of *sur* to signify a turning away from Yahweh and his ways.

The third of these words, *shuv(b)*, is used of "turning to or from" or of "returning to." Illustrative of this use is Isaiah 55:6–7. The prophet is urging Israel to turn back to the one from whom they have turned away.

Seek the LORD while he may be found;
  call on him while he is near.
Let the wicked forsake his way
  and the evil man his thoughts.
Let him turn (shuv) to the LORD, and he will have mercy on him,
  and to our God, for he will freely pardon.

Another passage illustrating this thesis is Jeremiah 3. The Lord is talking to the prophet about Judah and Israel, describing their relationship to him in marital terms. Israel and Judah are unfaithful wives who have broken their covenant of love. When God sees what Israel has done, he says: "I thought ... she would return (*shuv*) to me but she did not" (v. 7). Judah sees her sister's sin and decides to do the same. Despite the consequences that accompany her idolatry, Yahweh says: "Judah did not return (*shuv*) to me with all her heart, but only in pretense" (v.10). So Yahweh tells Jeremiah to go and proclaim this message:

"Return (shuv), faithless Israel" declares the LORD,
  "I will frown on you no longer,
for I am merciful," declares the LORD,
  "I will not be angry forever.
Only acknowledge your guilt...."

"Return (*shuv*), faithless people," declares the LORD, "for I am your husband." (vv. 12–14, emphasis added)

"I thought you would call me 'Father'
  and not turn (shuv) away from following me.
But like a woman unfaithful to her husband,
  so you have been unfaithful to me, O house of Israel,"
declares the LORD. (vv. 19–20)

Therefore, we should not be surprised when we find the Bible translation of the noun *shuvah* (a turning) as "repentance," because it is "a turning back": "In *repentance* and rest is your salvation, in quietness and trust is your strength" (Isa. 30:15, emphasis added). This meaning must be understood in contrast to the Greek understanding of repentance (*metanoia*), which literally means "a change of mind" or "an after-mind." For the Greek, the change can be simply a rational one. The Hebrew

CHAPTER 4: THE HUMAN PROBLEM   117

implies a change of relationship that is personal, not just cognitive. So Adam's sin was a turning away from the one from whose hand he came, the one who gave and sustained his life. Emil Brunner said it well: "The original ground and the original nature of sin is the severance of man from his origin, from the loving gracious and generous Word of God, which makes him free while it binds him, which gives him life in the very act of requiring it from him."[3]

THE RESULT OF HUMAN SIN

Cut Off from Our Source

Little wonder that Adam's world immediately went topsy-turvy. He himself was instantly diminished. Gabriel Marcel describes Adam's situation in philosophical terms: "The more exclusively it is I who exist, the less do I exist; and conversely, the more I free myself from the prison of ego-centricism, the more do I exist." He then describes the contrast: "The more my existence takes on the character of including others, the narrower becomes the gap which separates it from being; the more, in other words, I am."[4]

If we shut ourselves off from God, we will diminish ourselves because we have separated ourselves from those holy things that originate in him alone and for which we were made. To separate ourselves from our Source and Center means to implode on ourselves. The only power that can save us from collapsing in on ourselves is the presence of the Holy One, which alone can free us from the resulting bondage. But when we shut ourselves off from him, we shut ourselves off from others. The key to all other relationships is found in our relationship to God. If we are not open to God, we cannot properly be open to others. We will treat others the way we treat God. We will use them for our own advantage, not relating to them in true openness and holy-love. Ends will become means and means will become ends. We see this early on in Genesis in the relationship of the man and the woman.

Cut Off from Each Other

Adam, having detached himself from God, also detached himself psychologically from Eve because his center has become himself. He accuses her before God of being responsible for his own choice. Likewise, Eve, thinking defensively about herself, puts the blame for her own decision on someone else. Other-orientedness is replaced by self-interest, which manifests itself in rivalry, suspicion, distrust, fear of each other, and insecurity. The others in their lives become threats instead of sources of fulfillment. Adam and Eve treat each other as objects instead of as persons, means instead of ends, just as they can now put and keep God in the third person. Instead of the "Thou," which God is and ever should be, the loving "I Am" has now become for them the threatening "He Who Is."

Joe Sachs has caught a bit of the tragedy of this moment in his discussion of Genesis 6:5. His question is: How does one explain how a world, where everything is good and the original couple are living in unashamed transparency with each other and with God, becomes a world where every imagination of their thoughts is continually evil? Sachs explains it as simply a turning from the well-being of the whole to putting one's own good first. To do that one must be willing to sacrifice the other's good to his or her own interest. To use one another now seems legitimate. So Eve blames the serpent, and Adam blames Eve. Self-protection is the first concern. Trust has vanished. Sachs says: "Their response is the invention of clothes. They produce an imaginary safety, which is an outward sign of genuine inner barriers. Each has isolated himself by imagining how he might increase his own good at the expense of the other. It is to this new condition of solitary suspicion and distrust that their eyes are opened."[5]

Adam and Eve used fig leaves to cover themselves (Gen. 3:7). It was the Lord who made garments of skin for them (3:21). The thrust of the text seems to be that it was God's merciful act to give each one better protection from the other than they themselves could provide. Evil, and with it distrust and fear, had entered the fabric of human existence; every relationship now carried potential danger.

The two who had been made for God and for each other had now changed. God had said that it was not good for man to be alone. Now the one who said of his helper, "Bone of my bone and flesh of my flesh," considers whether it may not be safer to protect himself from what he has just called "flesh of my flesh." Now he puts his own good first and is willing to sacrifice his companion to it. Solipsism and autonomic individualism, our euphemisms for sin, find their origins in this story. Psychological separation and alienation become the ambiance in which the human creatures move. Both seek some protection from the other because each fears that the other is as untrustworthy as each now knows himself or herself to be.

God had told his couple that if they chose to know good and evil rather than simply a world of good, they would die the very day of that choice. The story tells us that after the choice they continued to live. Sach's comments, "If Adam and Eve before that day had lived a life as one flesh, then surely on that day they did die: they died as one being and were reborn as two."[6]

The separation–the breaking of their oneness, their communion–occurred. A world that was "very good" now became one in which separation, suspicion, distrust, fear, alienation, and self-interest reigned. And it all started when God's creatures decided that the human self should be central in a God-originated, God-centered, God-sustained, and God-determined world.

Living in the Flesh in Separation from God

Fallen humankind's orientation of themselves around themselves is so total and so universal that Paul can use the simple word *flesh* (*sarx*) as a metonym for the human problem that plagues us all. When he draws the distinction between the flesh and the Spirit and identifies the flesh as the source of all of our evil, there is no Greek dualism in his thinking. Life in the Spirit is what Adam and Eve knew in the garden before the fall. Life in the flesh for Paul is simply life lived out of our own resources and desires instead of out of the Spirit of God and his will. As Lesslie Newbigin says, "The words 'flesh' and 'Spirit' do not refer to parallel and analogous realities in our experience, such as 'visible' and 'invisible' or 'lower nature' and 'higher nature.'" *Flesh*, according to Newbigin and Paul, "denotes the whole of our creaturely being insofar as it seeks to organize itself and to exist in its own power apart from the continually renewed presence and power of God, 'from above.'"[7]

Humans apart from God become capable of all that is not good simply because they have shut themselves, in whole or in part, away from the source of all that is good, the Holy One, God. Humankind's problem is never because they have physical bodies. Nor is it because they have the limitations of finitude that go with their creatureliness. The proof of this is that God himself, the Holy One of Israel, has taken on human flesh with its creaturely limitations in the incarnation and maintains that flesh, redeemed, in his resurrected and ascended life.

So the flesh, for Paul, was not evil in itself. He believed that its moral character was determined by its relation to the Holy One. When human life was centered in the Holy One, flesh was suffused with God's own Spirit and the agape love that gave it a holy character. When separated from the source of all good and centered in itself, its gravitational bent was now in conflict with the nature of ultimate reality itself and thus destructive. Robert Jenson turns to Augustine for an understanding of this.

> Augustine has also an explanation for the incurvation of love, which is parallel to his explanation of the earthly city's subjection to the *libido dominandi*.... "In order to account for a ... native depravity of the heart of man, there is not the least need of supposing any evil quality ... *wrought* into the nature of man, by any *positive* cause ... either from God or the creature." All that is needed is for the supernatural presence of the Spirit not to be given, for created nature, following its own inevitabilities, to undo itself. "The inferior principles of self-love and natural appetite ... left to themselves, of course became reigning principles.... The immediate consequence of which was a turning upside down.... Man did immediately set up himself, and the objects of his private affections ... as supreme; and so they took the place of God."[8]

Little wonder that the New Testament pattern for the believer is the Spirit-filled, Spirit-led, Spirit-permeated, Spirit-controlled, and thus *other-oriented* person. Paul makes this quite clear in his Galatian letter when he speaks about our freedom in Christ. Centering ourselves in ourselves is not freedom. Paul taught that we are free only when we can live for one beyond ourselves, and that is possible only through the Spirit.

> You, my brothers, were called to be free. But do not use your freedom to indulge the sinful nature [the flesh]; rather, serve one another in love. The entire law is summed up in a single command: "Love your neighbor as yourself." If you keep on biting and devouring each other, watch out or you will be destroyed by each other.
>
> So I say, live by the Spirit, and you will not gratify the desires of the sinful nature [the flesh]. For the sinful nature [the flesh] desires what is contrary to the Spirit, and the Spirit what is contrary to the sinful nature [the flesh]. They are in conflict with each other, so that you do not do what you want. (5:13–17)

In his great passage on the death of Christ in 2 Corinthians 5, Paul explains that the person who is in Christ through the cross is a new creature who has died to his own will and does not live for himself, but lives for Christ. Paul sees this as the very purpose of the cross. "Christ's love compels us, because we are convinced that one died for all, and therefore all died. And he died for all, so that those who live should no longer live for themselves, but for him who died for them and was raised again" (vv. 14–15).

We need to be suffused with the Spirit, just as Jesus was, so we can be freed from the trammels of self and live with whole hearts for him. The pattern for us is seen in the life Jesus lived while he was here among us in the flesh. The pattern is not just a pattern for a religious or a moral/ethical life as we tend to think of it, but much more. It is the pattern for true personhood. To be a person is to be incomplete in oneself; therefore, no human person is complete who does not have the Spirit living within, releasing one from the self-interest that otherwise controls and binds. We must be free from what Jenson refers to as the self's "incurvation" so the self's "own inevitabilities" will not "undo itself." Paul is more graphic and blunt when he simply says: "To set the mind on the flesh is death, but to set the mind on the Spirit is life and peace. For this reason the mind that is set on the flesh is hostile to God; it does not submit to God's law—indeed it cannot, and those who are in the flesh cannot please God" (Rom. 8:6–8 NRSV).

Our completeness, our healthy personhood as it was created to be, is found not in ourselves, but *perichoretically* in God's Spirit. The person who knows that completeness is truly a new creature, a human as God intended the human creature to be.

The Reign of the "I"

Paul makes the distinction between life in the flesh and life in God's Spirit quite clear in his Roman letter. In his first chapter he begins to build his case that the world is under judgment because of its sin and evil (vv. 18–32). His word choice here is significant. The two factors underlying sin are *asebeia* and *adikia,* usually translated as "ungodliness" and "unrighteousness." These words are all-inclusive terms that contain within themselves all of the evil that follows. They are seen as largely synonymous in meaning. Etymologically, however, the words are quite distinct. The first comes from the Greek root *seb-,* which means "to reverence" or "to worship." Thus, it is a religious term by definition. The initial *a-* is a privative, which means that the person whose life is characterized by *asebeia* is not in a proper relationship of worship to God. The second term *adikia,* comes from the Greek root *dik-,* which means "right," from which the word *righteousness* develops. Again, the initial *a-* is a privative. So *adikia* as a result is an appropriate term to be used to describe generally all relationships that are not right, while *asebeia* is appropriate to speak of that condition in which one's relationship of worship and devotion toward God has been forfeited.

Paul is surely correct when he uses *asebeia* first and then speaks of *adikia.* He is consistent with a basic theme of all Scripture: Our relationships with others are not first of all what spoil our relationship with God. The fact is that our relationship with God is the key to all other relationships. When it is deficient, all other relationships go wrong. Biblically, we are told first to love God with all of our hearts and then to love our neighbors as ourselves. As David learned, sin is always first of all against God (Ps. 51:4). Thus *asebeia* is cause and *adikia* is result.

Proper worship is lost, and then everything else suffers inevitable damage. *Adikia* is a summary term that covers the long catalog of evils listed in the latter part of Romans 1, perhaps the most disheartening such catalog found in the Scriptures. But if God is the origin and only continuing source of all that is good and holy, how could this account of sinfulness in humanity be otherwise?

In a very perceptive way, Paul describes the downward journey of humankind from their Edenic beginning. In Romans 1:21 he explains that when people knew God they did not glorify him as God and were not thankful to him for life, for sustenance, or for his providential provision. Rather, humankind decided that a person's relationship to God could be separated from all other relationships, be neglected, and then ignored. The ontological center of all things could be forgotten, and one could build one's own world with self as the center. Life became a pretense and an illusion no longer properly related to reality, having its own negative impact on the intellectual life of the human creature. Human perception moved into the realm of fancy rather than reality. "Their thinking became futile and their foolish hearts were darkened" (v. 21).

Paul, a good Hebrew, used the term *heart* for the inner self where a person thinks, wills, and feels. Thus, the impact was total. The negative results were seen in the volitional activity and passions of a person as much as in the rational life. The relationship to God that gave order and freedom to human life was broken. As Augustine said, "The inferior principles of self-love and natural appetite ... left to themselves, of course became reigning principles."[9] All that had been centripetal in human existence was gone, and now the centrifugal reigned. Inevitably, all relationships were skewed. Disintegration replaced order. Appetites, creative and fulfilling when in holy order, now ruled over reason, and love turned into lust. Human passion, with its proper divine object gone, turned to created things. Natural human relationships, formerly fulfilling and freeing, were replaced by the unnatural with their accompanying bondage. Evil reigned because the proper tie with the Holy One had been broken.

For Paul, the paradigm for understanding our sin does not come first of all from Sinai. The context is not a burning mountain but a garden;

not the exodus but Eden. Law, as later seen in the Mosaic legislation, is not the central element. The determinative factor is the personal. Note Romans 1:28: "Furthermore, since *they did not think it worthwhile to retain the knowledge of God,* he gave them over to a depraved mind, to do what ought not to be done" (emphasis added). A personal relationship of loving trust was now replaced by distrust and a deep desire for distance from our Source and Sustainer. Man and woman have chosen to flee from their Friend. Their course now is one set against reality. Only tragedy can result.

This interpretation of Paul's thinking is confirmed in Romans 2:1–14. Paul's concern for the Gentile, as well as for the Jew, is eternal justice; God, the righteous Judge, will have the final word in human history. Paul can see two groups of people standing in that final day before God. The first is composed of those who seek glory, honor, and immortality. They will appropriately receive eternal life. The second group is composed of those who ultimately are objects of God's wrath. The explanation of why the second group reaches such a tragic position is given in one word: *eritheia* (v. 8).

That word represents a key concept for Paul. Confusion across the centuries about the true meaning of *eritheia* has made it more difficult to see the center of Paul's argument. Modern scholarship finally has established that the actual meaning is simply "base self-interest." Or, as the NIV and the NRSV translate it, "self-seeking." Friedrich Buchsel explains how the word developed from a term for the reward for a day's labor to a term for pure self-interest: "*Eritheia* is thus the attitude of self-seekers, harlots, etc., i.e., those who demeaning themselves and their cause are busy and active in their own interests, seeking their own gain or advantage."[10] The word is expression for such attitudes as "What's in it for me?" As such, it is the perfect word to describe the ego-centeredness of the person who has forbidden God to have the central place in his or her life. So Paul finds this single word strong enough to account for the wrath of God, which had concerned him in chapter 1 and will express itself on that final day in final judgment. The word *eritheia* speaks simply of the life lived out of oneself apart from God.

The development of human evil begins in the irreverence that displaces God from his rightful place in the human heart. With the true center gone, life is so centered in the self that it inevitably becomes destructive of all that is holy, just, and good. Paul's conclusion in Romans is that there are none of us who have not opted for this course, thereby creating the ultimate problems in our personal relationship with God. Paul describes quite graphically the origin of human troubles:

> Although they knew God, they neither glorified him as God nor gave thanks to him, but their thinking became futile and their foolish hearts were darkened.... Therefore God gave them over in the sinful desires of their hearts.... They exchanged the truth of God for a lie, and worshiped and served created things rather than the Creator....
> Because of this, God gave them over to shameful lusts....
> Furthermore, since they did not think it worthwhile to retain the knowledge of God, he gave them over to a depraved mind, to do what ought not to be done. (Rom. 1:21, 24–26, 28)

When sin is understood from a relational perspective, it is much easier to grasp that the way of salvation is a journey of faith. Sin began with doubt that quickened self-interest that resulted in un-love, disloyalty, rebellion, and death. So we are not surprised to find that the gospel claim is that the road back is the reverse. The end is faith, because faith produces the openness that makes possible reciprocal self-giving love. The road from that self-giving love to self-centeredness and rebellion began in a doubt leading to distrust and rejection. The way back is the reverse.

THE WAY OF SALVATION
IT IS ALL ABOUT THE NATURE OF GOD

five

This study began with the importance of the right concept of God, and we therefore started with Jesus. We found that beginning with Jesus brought us to a different understanding of God, an understanding based on his triune being as Father, Son, and Spirit, three divine persons united in one being in other-oriented, self-giving holy-love.

We also found that the very purpose of the creation was to invite us, God's creatures, to participate in the fellowship of other-oriented love that is the very life of God. This led to a different understanding of human personhood, one much richer than that traditionally acknowledged in the church. We learned that a person, even a divine person, is not complete in himself or herself. We learned that persons by definition always come in webs of relationships, and that it is in those relationships that a person finds his or her own identity and fulfillment. In a God-ordered universe no one lives to, from, or for oneself; the key to every person is in another. Persons are made to live in agape love. The reality that *perichoresis* reflects in the Godhead should have its analogical counterpart in our own human lives and enable us to understand how humankind began and the kind of existence God purposed for his creatures.

But when we had that privilege before the fall, we forfeited it by choosing a way of life contrary and hostile to the character of the life of

God. Whereas God is "Being-for-others," we chose to be "creatures-for-ourselves." Whereas "being-for-others" is the way of life and all good, "being-for-oneself" contains within it the seed of all that is evil and is the prelude to eternal death.

By rejecting God and his ways and choosing the path that could bring about the destruction of all of the good purposes of God, humankind found themselves alienated from God and under divine wrath. The harmony marking humanity's relationship to God and to one another was shattered. A creature made for love could now live only in alienation.

To use the metaphors of intimacy we discussed earlier, God found himself with a lawbreaker, a prodigal son, and an adulterous spouse on his hands. Rebellious humanity saw God's ways, the divine law, as challenges to be rejected, not a way of life to be internalized as God intended (Jer. 31:33; Ezek. 36:24–28). The Father was to be fled, not honored. And God was now replaced by ourselves in our affections. Self-love became the rule, rather than the other-love that was the very signature of God. The thoughts and imaginations of our hearts, along with the rejection of God and the good, became only evil (Gen. 6:5).

But how could this break in fellowship occur? Genesis 3 tells us that the betrayal began with a question that Satan posed to Eve: "Did God really say, 'You must not eat from any tree in the garden'?" (v. 1). Eve declared that God had only forbidden one tree, but then she studied the tree more closely and saw that its fruit was "good for food and pleasing to the eye, and also desirable for gaining wisdom" (v. 6). Suddenly Eve began to question the goodness of God, whether he was withholding something good from them. For the first time she considered the possibility *that something could be good in itself apart from God.* As a result, her question became a doubt. The doubt became distrust. Distrust quickly became distance and manifested itself in mechanisms for self-protection. Eve and her husband turned to hide themselves from the one who was the source of all goodness and of life itself. Their relationship of agape love with God was broken, and *eritheia*, or selfishness, reigned. The glory of God's presence was gone, and subsequent human history completes the story of their sin.

God himself was now beset with a tragic problem. A destructive virus was loose in his creation that had within it the power to pervert and destroy everything he made and to separate the creatures he loved from himself. All of his beneficent purposes for his creation were now threatened. Could he stand idly by and let his creation self-destruct? No! His sense of justice and his concern for his creatures demanded a response to the wrong, and his love did not permit him to stand aside while his own creation committed suicide. He had to step into the world that was made for freedom, deal with the evil, and stop the creation from destroying itself. As the judge of all the earth, he had to maintain the integrity of the order that his commands represent. Failure to do this would mean only total destruction. But, if he as Father were to save his creatures, he had to find a way to destroy the virus his creatures had released into his world and save the very ones responsible for its release. The possibility of an answer to the problem lay in the nature of personhood.

THE IMAGO DEI: PERSONHOOD

If we start with Jesus, we find that the incarnation and atonement were possible because human persons were made in the *imago Dei*, in the image of the divine persons. It was this likeness that enabled the second person of the Trinity to humble himself and come into our world as a human baby. His willingness to assume into himself all of the sin and hurt of the world enabled the possibility for fellowship between God and human persons to be restored. One of the marvels of personhood–human and divine–is the fact that persons come in webs of relationships. What happens in one person can make a difference in the possibilities of another. We are free creatures, so no one can make another's decisions, but what happens in one person can open doors for others. If we do not understand this truth, we will never understand the cross or the power of prayer in the Christian's life.

The openness of human personhood and the power of the self-giving love of God are obvious in the Old Testament where God is looking, not at his world, but at his own chosen people Israel, and finds them in hopeless rebellion. His justice demands that he punish them, but the punishment does not take them out of his heart. How can God be true to himself and also save his own people? He looks for a person. The problem is in persons. In fact, it started with a human person. So the answer has to be found where the problem is–not in God, but in the human persons he has created. There is nothing saving in them, but it is in these very creatures that the problem must be met. But how? God must find a counterpart to Adam. He needs a second Adam through whom redemptive forces, opposite to those set in motion by the original Adam, can be released to counter the sin that is there and overcome it.

The Old Testament gives us a number of passages, particularly in Isaiah, in which God looks for one to stand between him in his holiness and human persons in their sin. Isaiah 59 is perhaps the clearest. His answer is his own arm, "the arm of the LORD" (v. 1). "See, the Sovereign LORD comes with power, and his arm rules for him" (40:10). By his arm he carries out judgment on his people's enemy, Babylon (48:14). His arm will bring justice to the nations (51:5). The Lord swears by his arm and its power to execute his ultimate divine purposes (62:8). God's arm is his means of imposing his ways on creation. But, joy of joys, it also is his means of salvation (59:16). Deep as the problem is, the divine arm is perfectly adequate to solve it.

THE AIM OF THE LORD: JESUS, A NEW MODEL OF POWER

The arm of the Lord is the metaphor for the power of the Lord to save. However, we must be very careful in our interpretation of these passages as to what the nature of that power is. It is not the power to impose, nor a power by which the sovereign Lord solves the problem by decree or miraculous act. It is rather a power to take into himself the very problem that he longs to solve. Isaiah 53 gives us this astounding picture. There we find the identity of the "arm of the Lord." It is the suffering servant himself (v. 1). The offended one takes the offense into himself to save the one who offends. The physician assumes the very disease of the ones he has come to heal. The eternal Judge sentences himself to bear the very judgment that should go to the lawbreaker that stands before him. The Creator takes the place and the condemnation of the creature who has sinned against him.

Who has believed our message
    and to whom has the arm of the LORD been revealed?…
He was despised and rejected by men;
        a man of sorrows, and familiar with suffering.
Like one from whom men hide their faces
        he was despised, and we esteemed him not.

Surely he took up our infirmities
        and carried our sorrows;
yet we considered him stricken by God,
        smitten by him, and afflicted.
But he was pierced for our transgressions,
        he was crushed for our iniquities;
the punishment that brought us peace was upon him,
        and by his wounds we are healed.
All we, like sheep, have gone astray,
        each of us has turned to his own way;
And the LORD has laid on him
        the iniquity of us all.

… my righteous servant will justify many,
        and he will bear their iniquities.
… because he … was numbered with the transgressors.
For he bore the sin of many,
        and made intercession for the transgressors. (vv. 1, 3–6, 11, 12)

The arm of the Lord, the solution to the problem of our sin, is none other than Jesus himself, the son of Mary and the Son of God. When God could not find a human person through whom he could solve the human problem, he became one in his Son. Paul felt the glory of this: "For if the many died by the trespass of the one man, how much more did God's grace and the gift that came by the grace of the one man, Jesus Christ, overflow to the many!" (Rom. 5:15). "You see, at just the right time, when we were still powerless, Christ died for the ungodly.… But God demonstrates his own love for us in this: While we were still sinners, Christ died for us" (Rom. 5:6, 8). And in that sacrifice of himself, the one untouched by the curvature to self that has doomed us all, took upon himself our guilt and our sin–our curse–and made possible our deliverance from the sin that brought his death.

The only possibility for human salvation was for God's holy-love to enter into a human person, to incarnate itself in one of us. Therefore, the eternal Son, in whose likeness we were made, became one of us in Mary's boy. The triune nature of the being of God and the personal nature of the creature made it all possible. Only Christianity among the religions of the world is a religion of atonement; God himself can atone for the sins of his creatures. Such an incarnation and atonement can occur in no other religion because there is no other religion with a triune God and with the biblical understanding of personhood. In all other religions one's salvation must depend on one's own individual self. In Christianity salvation depends on God. That is, it is by God's grace alone.

THE WAY OF SALVATION: BEARING OTHERS

The key to our salvation obviously does not lie in us but in another. It rests in the one who gave himself for us. Our hope is in him and his capacity to take us and our sin into himself so that we can receive him and his saving life into ourselves. The language of salvation in the Old Testament speaks of this. The strongest Hebrew word for "forgive" in the Old Testament is the verb *nasa*, which means "to bear." One often does not know whether to translate it as "bear" or as "forgive." In Psalm 32:1 the psalmist describes the blessed person as one whose trespass is "forgiven" (lit., "borne") and to whom the Lord does not impute iniquity. One's blessedness finds its base, not in oneself, but in someone else.

The Old Testament language of *faith* presents a similar picture, even clearer than in the New Testament. Two families of words express faith and trust, whereas the New Testament has only one. In addition to the Hebrew *he'emin*, found in the Abraham story and elsewhere in the Old Testament, we also find the word *batach*, which occurs most often in the worship literature of the Old Testament, particularly in the Psalms. The former has within it the meaning to "confirm" or "support" and develops into the concept of confidence and faith. The second has more of the sense of "trust." In fact, in the Semitic cognate languages, it carries the thought of "lying extended upon" or "to repose oneself upon." Both words are used in the Old Testament to connote the fact that our hope is not in ourselves but in another, and that the only appropriate saving response is to cast ourselves upon that other. This kind of faith is not just faith in an abstract truth or a proposition, but faith in a person. The key for us is not in what we can do for ourselves, but in what another can and has done for us. Faith as personal trust opens the door to the reception of the saving grace found in the only one who is salvation. And all of this is possible because of the nature of personhood.

If the concept of personhood is helpful in understanding the necessity of the incarnation and the cross, it is also helpful in understanding the mystery of intercessory prayer. Prayer, and particularly intercession, constitutes for most of us one of the true mysteries of the Christian faith. Why do we need to pray for another? Does God not care more for the other person than we do? He certainly knows more about the need–any need–than we do. Does God need our help? Are his resources dependent on our assistance? If God is holy-love itself, do we need to twist his arm to persuade him to do good for someone else or for ourselves?

Further, why does God need to pray? Paul tells us in Romans 8:26 that the Holy Spirit, the third person of the divine Trinity, intercedes for us "with groans that words cannot express." Hebrews 7:25 insists that the eternal Son, the second person of the Godhead, "always lives to intercede" for those who approach God through him. Why does God need to pray?

THE INDWELLING CHRIST: AGAPE LOVE

Two factors shed light on the mystery of intercession: the nature of *perichoresis* and the power of agape love. *Perichoresis* and agape love can only be understood in terms of the interrelatedness of persons. The key to every person rests in another or in others. No person ever lives to himself alone. What happens in others determines our possibilities.

We see this primarily in Christ. What happens in Christ determines the possibilities for all of the rest of us. When he bore us in his heart on the cross, our options changed. The Scriptures indicate that this has wider applications. No human can atone for another's sins. No human can play God's part. He alone can ultimately change any of us. When one takes another or others into one's heart and the well-being of the other(s) becomes more important to the bearer than the bearer's own well-being, then, mystery of mysteries, possibilities open up for the one(s) borne that would not be there without the bearing. This is why Jesus could say to his disciples, "I will give you the keys of the kingdom of heaven; whatever you bind on earth will be bound in heaven, and whatever you loose on earth will be loosed in heaven" (Matt. 16:19). The context for that statement is the Caesarea Philippi conversation with the Twelve. Jesus insists that if they are to be his followers, their lives must also include a cross, just as his life, to effect salvation, had to end on Calvary (vv. 13–28). Jesus tells them that they must lose their lives to find them. They must die to themselves so that God can live in them. He means that they must lose their lives in something beyond themselves and for someone(s) beyond themselves. The history of the advance of the Christian church in a pagan world is filled with data to support the truthfulness and the effectiveness of this principle. For example, when John Knox said, "Give me Scotland, or I die," Scotland's possibilities changed.

A biblical example is found in the life of Moses. Taken into the pharaoh's house as an infant, he could have lived his life in that context with the privileges that went with it. But he saw the needs of his people, which called for his flight and a radical change of circumstances and lifestyle. Then came the call from God. From the experience of God's word and presence at the burning bush, Moses set his face to live, sometimes unwillingly, for his people. In a sense, his life was one of intercession, verbal and otherwise, for Israel. When the people grumbled and complained against God, Moses prayed, and the fire of God's judgment was stopped (Num. 11:1–3). When Aaron and Miriam spoke against their brother, slandering him, God inflicted Miriam with leprosy. Moses' intercession for his critically ill sister made possible her cleansing (Num. 12:1–16). What happened inside Moses had a determining effect on Israel's possibilities. Moses surrendered his own life for the sake of a nation and for the blessing of the world. The key to the power in his life seems without question to be the fact that he was more concerned about Israel's well-being than he was his own (Ex. 32:32).

Again, there is no way a person can force changes in another's life. That power does not rest in us. No one can make another's decisions, but in the mystery of the nature of the divine image and the co-inherent character of interpersonal relations, the key to a person's possibilities lies in someone else. This helps us to understand the power of good in the lives of the beneficent saints who have marked history. They have had more than intellectual or psychological influence on the church; they have had an existential influence that has affected the possibilities of choice in other persons. The nature of love is other-oriented, self-giving, and sacrificial. It is born in our spirits by God himself, who is love.

The physical world has its counterpart in human birth. We are all here because someone else carried us in her body until we were born. The language to describe intercession is the same: The mother *bears* the child; the birth experience is *travail*, as likewise those who pray are said to "bear" and "labor." Of course, the physical is only analogical to the spiritual. There is mystery in both arenas–the physical and the spiritual. The reality is that, when a Christian lets God put within him or her God's own concern for a friend, family, church, institution, or even a country, spiritual possibilities develop that otherwise would not exist. Paul seems to have counted on the effectiveness of this "bearing." He can say to those for whom he feels a spiritual responsibility, "My dear children ... I am again in the pains of childbirth until Christ is formed in you" (Gal. 4:19). Paul obviously felt that what happened in him was important for those for whom he was responsible. He also saw a potential in those to whom he was writing, for he urges the Galatians to "carry [bear] each other's burdens, and in this way you will fulfill the law of Christ" (6:2). There is saving potential in the *perichoretic* nature of personhood. Paul staked his life on it.

FULFILLMENT OF SALVATION

PERFECT LOVE

Our study has enabled us to see that the nature of sin was in the beginning the perversion of a personal relationship with a personal God. A relationship of intimate, loving trust became one of doubt, distance, and disobedience. Humans chose to turn their relationship of other-oriented, self-giving love into a self-centered inversion ("incurvature," to use the phrase of Augustine, Luther, Nygren, and others). They made themselves the center of their own existence, their primary point of reference, displacing God, who is the loving Source and Sustainer of all. Humans decided to establish their own kingdom within the self where they could reign unchallenged.

God thus found his creatures, ones to whom he longed to betroth himself, choosing to rebel within the Father's house, giving themselves to other loves. Passions that were made to bind people to God and to others were now turned away from their intended objects and focused on the selfish concerns of the creature, on everything but God. Life was now so oriented around self that the word *flesh* became a metonym for human life out of the will of its Maker. Humankind defiled everything they touched because they were not capable of any act not stained by self-interest, the essence of sin. Paul says that all have sinned. Human glory, once a reflection of God's glory, is gone (Rom. 3:23).

God, who is love, has acted to redeem us, and this redemption fits the picture we have discovered. Christ's sacrifice of himself–the just for the unjust–meets the demands of the royal/legal metaphor. This metaphor has been a very important one in the history of Christian thought, often serving as the primary approach to our understanding of sin and atonement. Paul establishes the importance of this understanding in Romans 3:21–26 where he explains the death of Christ as God's putting forward Christ "as a sacrifice of atonement, through faith in his blood" (v. 25) for our sins so we may stand justified before God. The atonement made possible the forgiveness of our sins. The penalty for our sin has been paid in Christ's blood, and reconciliation with God has been offered us in Christ.

The church, particularly the Protestant church, in its better moments has been quite clear in its perception of the nature of sin and salvation from the perspective of this metaphor. But understanding the character of the relationship that God desires with humans requires more than is found in the one metaphor. If the conditions necessary for the fulfillment of God's demands were met in Christ's death for us, then the gospel is bigger and better than we have often thought. Christ died to offer more for his church than we often recognize.

IT IS MORE THAN FORGIVENESS

The need of sinners constitutes more than our common understanding of forgiveness and justification provides. The sin that permeates us is too deep, and the perverted twist it has produced in our human psyche is too profound. We need much more than another chance. We need a radical change in our nature, and that cannot come from us. We need, as it were, to be born all over again with a new life, divine life, the passions of which are directed to something and Someone beyond ourselves. Our passions need cleansing and redirection. We need an infusion of that holy-love that moves the heart of God, a love that can reverse the "incurvation." We need the other-oriented, self-giving love that was God's original plan for us.

The family metaphor provides the context for part of God's plan. Paul speaks joyously to Titus of the goodness and loving-kindness of God that has provided in Christ not only the possibility of a pardon for our sins, but of a new birth in which the Spirit makes us new creatures and begins a new life, the very life of God, within us (Titus 3:4–7). The sign of this new birth is that the holy-love of God, agape love, is poured into our hearts (Rom. 5:5). The tyranny of our self-absorption is broken. John can say to those to whom he writes: "How great is the love (*agape*) the Father has lavished on us, that we should be called children of God! And that is what we are!" (1 John 3:1).

God through Christ has come again to live in the heart of his creature, and with the divine presence comes the holy-love that characterizes the divine nature. The proof of the change is twofold. First, the inner person experiences a consciousness of reconciliation and of belonging again to the Father. This is the witness of the Spirit to our forgiveness and adoption (Rom. 8:15–26; 1 John 3:1–2). And, second, a conscious change in our concerns arises out of the new life within us. We experience a rush of love, agape love, the evidence of the divine life now born within us, for someone other than ourselves, for God and others (2 Cor. 5:14–15).

A change begins to take place in the direction toward which the inner self turns. A new point of reference is established and begins to replace the old center of the self. Christ begins to make his claim within us for the position that is rightfully his and which he has lost–his position as the determining center of the inner self, his position as Lord. The Spirit within us begins to show us the depth of the "incurvation" that has bound and defiled us. Through his influence, we begin to see the nature of the "mind of the flesh" of which Paul speaks and its hostility to the God who has redeemed us. The process of our sanctification has begun. We now have the freedom to begin to choose God instead of surrendering to our own tyrannous desires. As our new life comes from the Spirit, we are now to live (the Greek text uses the metaphor of "keeping in step" or "walking") in the Spirit (Gal. 5:25). The purpose of the Spirit within us is to bring us to the place of which Paul speaks when he says of himself, "I no longer live, but Christ lives in me. The life I live in the body, I live by faith in the Son of God, who loved me and gave himself for me" (Gal. 2:20).

Paul can even say of himself that his hearers should take him as their example (1 Cor. 4:16–17). His confidence is strong enough that he can say from the Roman jail to his friends at Philippi: "For to me, to live is Christ" (Phil. 1:21).

The purpose of the Spirit in the life of the new believer is to bring the person as a part of the bride of Christ to a devotion to Christ that fulfills the demands implicit within the nuptial metaphor, demands better expressed through that figure than through either the royal/legal or familial metaphor. The relationship sought is one of total self-giving love whereby the two belong to each other in a union so complete that to touch one is to touch the other. What the Spirit seeks is a relationship of love in which Christ reigns supreme without rival or competitor as Lord and Lover within the believer. It is the relationship longed for in the ancient collect used to prepare the believer for the reception of Holy Communion:

> Almighty God, unto whom all hearts are open, all desires known, and from whom no secrets are hid; cleanse the thoughts of our hearts by the inspiration of thy Holy Spirit, that we may perfectly love thee and worthily magnify thy holy name; through Christ our Lord. Amen.

IT IS ALL ABOUT AN UNDIVIDED HEART

This relationship begins in the experience of justification and new birth but is not completed there. The history of the church, as well as the biblical narrative, make it evident that justification and new birth in themselves do not assure such a relationship of pure love and an undivided heart, although they are the basis for the possibility. So when does one reach the point where one's love for Christ is the central and the all-controlling passion of one's life? When does the love of Christ reign without challenge within our inner spirits, and when are we wholly his? Do these questions point to an ideal we seek but that always will be just beyond our grasp in this life?

Too often in the history of the church, the belief that such a love is possible in the here and now has either been ignored or denied. Yet the Scriptures tell us that from the earliest days of Israel's existence, God's desire for his people has been that they should love him with an unmixed devotion. Yahweh sought in Israel a bride who would love him with an undivided heart: "The LORD your God will circumcise your hearts and the hearts of your descendants, so that you may love him with all your heart and with all your soul, and live" (Deut. 30:6).

The story of Israel is the repetitive story of a nation with a wandering eye and an adulterous spirit. God's response was thus one of displeasure and ultimate judgment. The New Testament picks up the motif of the undivided heart. Jesus speaks of it in terms of the pure heart (Matt. 5:8), the opposite of an adulterous one. Jesus even insists that such a heart is the requisite condition for seeing God. He clearly tells a scribe who inquires about the greatest of the commandments that loving God with all one's heart, mind, and soul and one's neighbor as oneself is the primary demand of the divine law (Mark 12:28–34). The implication of the passage is that such a thing is not beyond possibility but presently attainable.

Paul develops the theme of death to sin and resurrection to a new life in the Spirit (Rom. 6:1–4). He sees Christian baptism as picturing a death to our old patterns and a resurrection to a new one. The new life the resurrected person lives is in the Spirit and not in the "flesh" (Rom. 8:1–15). The law is fulfilled through divine agape love (Rom. 12:9–15), which the Spirit pours into our inner being (Rom. 8:3–4; 13:8–10). Such a life in which Jesus is actually Lord is possible through the Spirit whom God puts within the circumcised heart of the believer (1 Cor. 12:3). But is such a life to be reserved for the *eschaton*? Do we actually have a record of anyone ever really receiving it in this life?

We certainly have a record of plenty who did not. We have only to look at Israel through its history to see God's own chosen people, most of whom did not. And in the first-century church we find the same. Paul indicates as much in his Philippian letter. He is in prison in Rome for his faith. His imprisonment has challenged some of his fellow believers to a more open confession of their faith. However, some are proclaiming Christ with mixed motives. Some who are not too fond of Paul are preaching Christ from motives of envy and rivalry, hoping, as Paul says, to add to his burdens (Phil. 1:15–18). He says they are moved by "selfish ambition" (v. 17). The Greek word here is significant; it is the same word encountered in Romans 2:8–*eritheia* ("self-interest"). On the other hand, others in Rome are challenged by Paul's faithfulness and are preaching Christ out of agape love, love untainted by self-interest (Phil. 1:16).

So there are two different kinds of believers in Rome. Paul desires to send someone to Philippi to check on the state of the church there. Unfortunately, he can find only one in his team who is prepared to go–Timothy. The others, Paul says, are concerned about their own interests. The Greek text literally says, "For everyone looks out for his own interests [lit., 'seeks the things of themselves'], not those of Jesus Christ" (Phil. 2:21). The fact that they were believers did not mean they were free from the contamination of *eritheia*. Timothy had found that freedom (vv. 19–23). Paul describes such liberty as having the "mind of Christ" since, as we have seen previously, Christ never sought his own interests but those of others. Paul quotes a hymn about the mind of Christ in Philippians 2:5–11. His introduction to the hymn is an admonition to the Philippians: "Do nothing from selfish ambition (*eritheia*) or conceit, but in humility regard others as better than yourselves. Let each of you look not to your own interests, but to the interests of others. Let the same mind be in you that was in Christ Jesus" (vv. 3–5 NRSV).

The letter to the Philippians gives us a very interesting picture of a first-century church some three decades after the ascension of Christ. This church seems to be Paul's favorite. His affection and respect for them are obvious in his words to them. They may well have represented first-century Christianity at its best. Yet not all of the believers in Philippi, as in Paul's team, were alike. Some were still troubled by a divided loyalty that hindered the devotion Paul yearned to see in his churches. Others seemed to have found victory over the inner contamination of self-interest. At least, as Paul says, Timothy had. Christ and the needs of the church came before Timothy's concern for himself. Self had been subordinated to Christ.

But how did Timothy escape that defilement? Was he a nobler sort? Was he naturally a more religious and more gracious kind of person? If that is the answer, we would need to conclude that we are not all equally sinful and that we can escape from our sin other than through divine grace. Paul would never have made such a claim. He knew better. But if Timothy found freedom from that inner sin through grace—God's answer to our sin—then such freedom must be possible for others, because God is no respecter of persons.

The situation in Philippi makes one think of a similar situation in the church at Corinth. Paul tells the Corinthian believers that he cannot speak to them as he would to spiritual people because they are infants in Christ. He must feed them with the simpler things of the gospel, for they are not ready for "solid food." Their lives are still plagued by what he calls in Galatians "works of the flesh." Jealousy and quarreling mar their fellowship. Their life is still marked by the carnal, the fleshly, because they have not let Christ lead them into life in the fullness of the Spirit (see 1 Cor. 3). The King James translation is particularly clear.

> For ye are yet carnal: for whereas there is among you envying, and strife, and divisions, are ye not carnal, and walk as men? For while one saith, I am of Paul; and another, I am of Apollos; are ye not carnal? Who then is Paul, and who is Apollos, but ministers by whom ye believed, even as the Lord gave to every man? I have planted, Apollos watered; but God gave the increase. So then neither is he that planteth anything, neither he that watereth; but God that giveth the increase. Now he that planteth and he that watereth are one.... For we are labourers together with God. (1 Cor. 3:3-9)

The unity of the body of Christ has been broken by self-centeredness, the very essence of sin. But Paul gives no indication that this condition is inescapable. In fact, he goes to some length in 1 Corinthians to explain that God has delivered him personally from just such a condition. He urges the Corinthian believers to seek such freedom.

The Corinthian letters are pastoral letters. Paul directly addresses problems within the body of Corinthian believers. One of those is the matter of Christian liberty, to what degree a believer's scruples should be binding. There is considerable difference, for instance, within the Corinthian community on questions of food purchased in the public markets. Paul knows that a person's salvation is not determined by what one eats. So he insists that he does not have to be bound by the legalistic understanding of another believer. But he also insists that his rights must be subject to Christ. Love dictates that he cannot be a cause of stumbling to his "weaker" brother, who is not yet as enlightened and mature as he is. To do so would be to sin, not only against the weaker brother, but against Christ himself.

> Take care that this liberty of yours does not somehow become a stumbling block to the weak. For if others see you, who possess knowledge, eating in the temple of an idol, might they not, since their conscience is weak, be encouraged to the point of eating food sacrificed to idols? So by your knowledge those weak believers for whom Christ died are destroyed. But when you thus sin against members of your family, and wound their conscience when it is weak, you sin against Christ. Therefore, if food is a cause of their falling, I will never eat meat, so that I may not cause one of them to fall. (1 Cor. 8:9–13 NRSV)

The well-being of those whom Paul carried in his heart took priority over the exercise of his own rights. The divine agape love within his heart meant that the Corinthian believers' salvation was far more important to him than the freedom implicit within his rights. In fact, concerning his rights in Christ he says the following:

> We have not made use of this right, but we endure anything rather than put an obstacle in the way of the gospel of Christ....
> I have made no use of any of these rights.... What then is my reward? Just this: that in my proclamation I may make the gospel free of charge, so as not to make full use of my rights in the gospel.
> For though I am free with respect to all, I have made myself a slave to all, so that I might win more of them.... I

have become all things to all people, that I might by all means save some. I do it all for the sake of the gospel, so that I may share in its blessings. (1 Cor. 9:12, 15, 18–19, 22–23 NRSV)

Paul obviously has found freedom from the defiling tyranny of his own desires. He is free to surrender his rights and privileges to the lordship of Christ and to do it joyously. More significant for our discussion is that he clearly feels that the Corinthians should let God give them the same freedom. He is citing himself not as an example of exceptional piety, but rather an example of what the Holy Spirit wants to do in washing every human heart clean through the blood of Christ. He is longing for his Corinthian friends to know this freedom. So he says: "'All things are lawful,' but not all things are beneficial. 'All things are lawful,' but not all things build up. Do not seek your own advantage, but that of the other" (1 Cor. 10:23–24 NRSV).

His conclusion is both admonition and testimony: "So, whether you eat or drink, or whatever you do, do everything for the glory of God. Give no offense to Jews or to Greeks or to the church of God, just as I try to please everyone in everything I do, not seeking my own advantage, but that of many, so that they may be saved. Be imitators of me, as I am of Christ" (1 Cor. 10:31–11:1 NRSV).

Such thinking was not occasional or exceptional for Paul, but it permeated and at times was the capstone of all his correspondence. He begins his closing portion of Romans with very similar language:

We who are strong ought to bear with the failings of the weak and not to please ourselves. Each of us should please his neighbor for his good, to build him up. For even Christ did not please himself but, as it is written: "The insults of those who insult you have fallen on me." For everything that was written in the past was written to teach us, so that through endurance and the encouragement of the Scriptures we might have hope.

May the God who gives endurance and encouragement give you a spirit of unity among yourselves as you follow Christ Jesus, so that with one heart and mouth you may glorify the God and Father of our Lord Jesus Christ. (15:1–6)

Paul's message and witness have a remarkable consistency. He insists that Christ came to deliver us, the work of his hands, from the twistedness of our sin that has turned us in on ourselves. We are unable to live as he intended us to live as the persons of the Godhead themselves live–in self-giving holy agape love. When Paul writes to the Philippians, he affirms that for him to live is Christ (1:21). To the Galatians he says he has been crucified with Christ so the life he now lives is not his own but is Christ himself living within him (2:20). To the Romans he insists that his readers should not please themselves because Christ did not please himself (15:2–3).

Regardless of which letter one reads, the pattern to be followed is the same: Jesus in his incarnation and passion. Jesus was a human person the way a human person is supposed to be. He came not to do his own will but that of his Father! So as he faced the cross he could say: "Yet not what I will, but what you will" (Mark 14:36 et al.). Paul himself has come through grace to a similar place. He obviously believes that the same Spirit who enabled Christ and who has transformed him can likewise transform his hearers and readers. How is it possible? Not by human nobility, piety, or self-discipline. It is all of grace. And if by grace, it is to be received by faith. Thus, Paul concludes his comments to the Galatians on this new life in Christ with the poignant and telling words: "I do not nullify the grace of God" (2:21 NRSV).

THE ROLE OF THE SPIRIT

Christ died to do more for us than get us past the judgment. He died to give us the freedom of which Paul speaks, and he now waits for us to accept it. We as sinners must come to realize that we can never atone for our sins, and we must trust Christ to do for us what we cannot do for ourselves. We must also let the Spirit of holiness cleanse our inner persons as Christians from the defilement of self-interest, realizing this is beyond our capacity to accomplish. Thus, we must trust the Spirit to do for us what we cannot do for ourselves. The power to live the life Christ wants us to live is found only in the divine gift of God's own agape love. Salvation always and everywhere at any stage of human existence is purely a gift to be received by faith. When Peter reported to the Jerusalem Council in Acts 15 on the coming of the Spirit to the household of the devout Cornelius, he said: "God, who knows the heart, showed that he accepted them by giving the Holy Spirit to them, just as he did to us. He made no distinction between us and them, for he purified their hearts by faith" (vv. 8–9). Apparently the fire of the Spirit at Pentecost was a cleansing fire that was received by faith.

Christ's atoning blood and the inner working of the Holy Spirit have power to cleanse the heart of the believer to its innermost depths and bring the believer to the place where Christ is the supreme and reigning love of his or her life. So why are the history of the church and the lives of most Christian believers full of strife and division? Is it not because the possibility of a heart controlled by the pure love of Christ has been largely inconceivable? The fact that we have not thought it possible has not kept us from yearning for it. A surprising amount of the devotional literature of the church speaks to this issue. The church's hymnody particularly addresses it. Note the cry of the learned Anglican divine Edwin Hatch. His yearning was for the purity of an undivided will.

> *Breathe on me, Breath of God;*
> *Fill me with life anew,*
> *That I may love what thou dost love,*
> *And do what thou wouldst do.*
>
> *Breathe on me, Breath of God,*
> *Until my heart is pure,*
> *Until with thee I will one will,*
> *To do and to endure.*
>
> *Breathe on me, Breath of God,*
> *Till I am wholly thine,*
> *Until this earthly part of me*
> *Glows with thy fire divine.*
>
> *Breathe on me, Breath of God;*
> *So shall I never die,*
> *But live with thee the perfect life*
> *Of thine eternity.*[1]

George Matheson, a Scot, used a different figure, but his cry was the same. He longed to be so captured by the love of God that the inner resistance of a divided will would be overcome. Only then could he really be free.

> *Make me a captive, Lord,*
> *And then I shall be free;*
> *Force me to render up my sword,*
> *And I shall conqueror be.*
> *I sink in life's alarms*
> *When by my self I stand;*
> *Imprison me within Thine arms,*
> *And strong shall be my hand.*
>
> *My heart is weak and poor*
> *Until it Master find.*
> *It has no spring of action sure;*
> *It varies with the wind.*
> *It cannot freely move*
> *Till Thou hast wrought its chain.*
> *Enslave it with Thy matchless love,*
> *And deathless it shall reign.*
>
> *My power is faint and low*
> *Till I have learned to serve;*
> *It wants the needed fire to glow,*
> *It wants the breeze to nerve.*
> *It cannot drive the world*
> *Until itself be driv'n.*
> *Its flag can only be unfurled*
> *When Thou shalt breathe from heav'n.*
>
> *My will is not my own*
> *Till thou hast made it Thine;*
> *If it would reach a monarch's throne*
> *It must its crown resign.*
> *It only stands unbent,*

Amid the clashing strife;
When on Thy bosom it has leant
And found in Thee its life.[2]

These prayers are obviously those of believers of some maturity and understanding. Who among those of us who have come to know the touch of divine grace within our hearts has not found these hymns a true expression of our deepest longings? And who has not known that such longings are the result of the wooing work of the Holy Spirit?

But has the Spirit put such hungers within us merely to taunt us? Or are these hungers themselves a work of God's Spirit, God's way of telling us that he has made possible a deeper cleansing for us through the one who bears us on the cross and in his resurrection and who gives to us the gift of his Spirit? Are we ready to say that the Holy Spirit, through the blood of Christ, cannot take the spiritual adultery from our hearts, or as John says, "perfect our hearts in love" so that we can love Christ with all of our hearts?

Apparently John was not ready to concede such. His word, like that of Peter at the Jerusalem conference in Acts 15:8, is a promise of cleanness: "But if we walk in the light, as he is in the light, we have fellowship with one another, and the blood of Jesus, his Son, purifies us from all sin" (1 John 1:7). John is not talking here of forgiveness or justification. He is speaking to fellow believers. His concern in this verse is not our status before God but our inner heart condition. He projects a picture for us of a person who is fully open in unobstructed and unbroken communion with Christ and who finds the power of the divine presence through that sacrificial offering of the Son able to unite and purify the heart. *Unbroken, unobstructed communion is the answer to the divided heart.* Such an outcome cannot be the result of human works, for our sin is so deep and pervasive that even our efforts to remove it are contaminated by our sinfulness. Only God can cleanse our hearts.

IT IS ALL A GIFT TO BE RECEIVED: HIS FULLNESS

Our sanctification, then, just like our justification, is a work of grace, a work of God–a pure gift from the loving hand of the Father.

Therefore, the necessary key is faith. We must believe in God enough to entrust ourselves entirely to his tender care. In his Galatian letter, preliminary to his remarks on life in the Spirit, Paul says of our liberty in Christ: "For in Christ Jesus neither circumcision nor uncircumcision has any value. The only thing that counts is faith expressing itself through love" (5:6). Our work, religious or otherwise, can satisfy neither our own heart nor the heart of God. But the Spirit works through faith, making it possible for him to pour into our hearts the agape love that satisfies our longings and enables the fulfillment of the law in us.

Paul writes to the Romans a few years before the destruction of the temple in Jerusalem. He envisions a service to God that will take the place of that which has been the center of Israel's worship since Moses. In the worship that he is envisioning, the believer's sacrifice is not the bodies of animals, but the very person of the worshiper. It is to be holy and acceptable to God and will bring grace to the worshiper that will enable that person to discern and do the good, acceptable, and perfect will of God (12:1–2).

The grace that such a sacrifice of self brings is nothing other than the gift of the very *agape love of God.* For four chapters (Romans 12–15) Paul gives content to the meaning of this gift for a person's life. His argument about the nature of the gospel is a symphony with a major theme: agape love that does not seek the things of itself. It is other-oriented. It is Christ's love: "We who are strong ought to bear with the failings of the weak and not to please ourselves. Each of us should please his neighbor for his good, to build him up. For even Christ did not please himself but, as it is written: 'The insults of those who insult you have fallen on me'" (15:1–3).

Paul began his letter by boasting of the power of God to save us from our sinfulness. Here in his closing chapters of Romans, he pictures the nature of that salvation as it works its way out in our individual lives in the body of Christ. In other words, the sacrifice of Christ was to restore to the human heart the glory, the agape love, the divine presence that we lost in the fall.

Note Paul's picture of the effects of this gift of love:

The ones who are full of agape love do not think of themselves more highly than they ought to think. They think soberly, recognizing that they are members of a body larger than any individual one of them (12:3–5).

They honor each other more than themselves in mutual devotion to one another (12:10).

They bless those who persecute them and do not curse. Nor do they avenge themselves. They feed their enemies and give drink to those that are thirsty (12:14–20).

They submit to the authorities over them (13:1–7).

They hold no debts except to love one another. They love their neighbors as themselves and thus fulfill the Law (13:8–10).

They do not live for themselves, but for the Lord (14:7–8).

They live to please their neighbors, just as Christ did not live to please himself but to bring grace and blessing to others (15:1–3).

Paul himself is an example of this kind of love. He has spent his life sacrificially giving the gospel to others. Now he is carrying a financial offering to the church in Jerusalem for the poor who are in its midst. He is on his way to Spain to share the gospel with those who have never heard the Good News. He has lived, is living, and will live his life for Christ and others (Rom. 15:23–32). Those who are followers of Christ and who have received this divine love do not live to please themselves. So Paul urges his fellow believers in Rome: "Rather, clothe yourselves with the Lord Jesus Christ, and do not think about how to gratify the desires of the sinful nature" (13:14).

Paul knows that what he is proposing is not possible for the natural person. He is pointing to an experience in which Christ enters us and we enter into Christ so that he can speak of our being clothed with him. Then what is not possible naturally becomes possible because Christ and his Spirit dwell within us. Paul is urging his readers to enter and to live in just such a relationship with God. He is not suggesting that such a life lived in love is for some future age. His message is that it is for the present rather than an ideal about which to dream. It is a possibility in grace because it is not a matter of attainment. Such love is a gift that can only be received. It is a gift because it is the very life of God himself. One does not rise to such a life. One kneels to receive, to let him who is agape love fill and complete our personhood.

One can legitimately ask, "Why doesn't this deep cleansing come at the time of our justification and new birth?" The Bible makes it quite clear that such cleansing did not come to every believer whose story it records. Even with our Lord's disciples, in spite of their intimacy with Christ, the change did not come immediately. It was after Jesus began to speak to his disciples about the cross that the full extent of their self-centeredness manifested itself more fully.

Mark pictures this behavior for us quite clearly in his account of the story of the journey from Caesarea Philippi to Jerusalem (Mark 8–15). As Jesus began to try to prepare his disciples for the cross, he told them that there would be a cross for them as well. Chapters 8–10 give a remarkable picture of the self-interest that was still in their hearts, a self-interest that ultimately led the strongest of the Twelve to deny the Lord three times. Perhaps the point that Mark and the other evangelists are making is that many of us have to live with Christ and learn the inner checkings of the Spirit before we see the depths of our need for cleansing if we are to live lives that are truly holy.

The reality is that we will not trust God to do something for us if we do not feel the need. As we walk with him and expose ourselves to the Scriptures and to the constraints of the Holy Spirit, we begin to sense the inner division in the depths of our being that springs from an existential fear of totally trusting ourselves to his control. That fear of surrender to God, who loves us more than he loves himself, is the final evidence of our fallen sinfulness.

If we fully face the claims of Scripture about the possibilities of grace, we begin to hunger for that deeper cleansing and filling of God's Spirit, the very Spirit that first shed the love of God within our hearts. To be filled with the Spirit, of course, is to be filled with that very love of God. Then we do not fear his total control over us but welcome it because we welcome the God who is agape love itself. This, it seems, is what John is talking about when he says: "There is no fear in love. But perfect love drives out fear, because fear has to do with punishment. The one who fears is not made perfect in love" (1 John 4:18). The passion of believers' lives then is to let God give us this love and then let him fill us. John Wesley expressed this poignantly when he wrote the following:

> Love is the highest gift of God; humble, gentle, patient love.... It were well that you should be sensible of this, "the heaven of Heavens is love." There is nothing higher in religion, there is in effect, nothing else; if you look for anything but more love, you are looking wide of the mark, you are getting out of the royal way. And when you are asking others, "Have you received this or that blessing?" if you mean anything but more love, you mean wrong; you are leading them out of the way, putting them upon a false scent. Settle it then in your heart, that from the moment God has saved you from all sin, you are to aim at nothing more, but more of that love described in the thirteenth of the Corinthians. You can go no higher than this, till you are carried into Abraham's bosom.[3]

Why is there nothing higher than love? Wesley understood just as John before him did. There is nothing higher than agape love because that is what God is, and he offers himself to any who will receive him. What a gospel, and it is for the likes of me!

NOTES

CHAPTER 1: A NEW CONCEPT OF GOD

1. Yehezkel Kaufmann, *The Religion of Israel*, trans. Moshe Greenberg (Chicago: University of Chicago Press, 1960), 486.
2. Kaufmann insists that the uniqueness of Israel's religion lies in its concept of the divine. For Kaufmann the religion of Israel understands God to be one who "is supreme over all. There is no realm above or beside him to limit his absolute sovereignty. He is utterly distinct from, and other than, the world; he is subject to no laws, no compulsions, or powers that transcend him. He is, in short, non-mythological. This is the essence of Israelite religion, and that which sets it apart from all forms of paganism" (ibid., 60). By *paganism* Kaufmann means all religions other than Judaism, Islam, and Christianity.
3. In his book *Called to Be Holy*, John Oswalt gives a strikingly clear and helpful analysis of the differences between the biblical worldview and the alternative options in the ancient world and in our own. The distinctions established in his work are basic to all that follows here. See John N. Oswalt, *Called to Be Holy* (Nappanee, Ind.: Evangel, 1999), 10–14.
4. Maimonides, *The Guide of the Perplexed*, trans. Shlomo Pines (Chicago: University of Chicago Press, 1963), 609.
5. The term *other-oriented* will occur some thirty times in this book. This is an intentional attempt to describe the essence of true personhood, human and divine. I have found no better word to describe the nature of divine personhood and the intended nature of human personhood.
6. Later we will deal with the fact that the fall took from us this other-orientedness and left us centered in ourselves. An inversion occurred in the fall that affected, not only what a human could *do*, but also what a human, without the assistance of the Holy Spirit, could *think*.
7. Brian L. Horne, "Art: A Trinitarian Imperative?" in *Trinitarian Theology Today*, ed. Christopher Schwobel (Edinburgh: T. & T. Clark, 1995), 87–88.
8. Oswalt, *Called to Be Holy*, 90.
9. Walter Kasper, *The God of Jesus Christ* (New York: Crossroad, 1996), 309.
10. This practice became so universal and was followed for so long that the original spelling and pronunciation were lost. Not knowing how it was accurately spelled or pronounced, knowing only the four consonants in the original name,

the Jews came to refer to it as the "Tetragrammaton," the "Four Letter Word"– *YHWH*. Much of later Judaism has maintained this fear of misusing the holy name. As a result, the word *God* is often spelled in Jewish literature "G-D" to indicate the writer's respect and fear of offending Yahweh. The orthodox Jew who comes upon the Tetragrammaton when reading the biblical text will even today carefully insert the word *Lord* for God's name.

CHAPTER 2: THE LEVEL OF INTIMACY GOD DESIRES

1. Louis Berkhof, *Manual of Reformed Doctrine* (Grand Rapids: Eerdmans, 1933), 257.
2. John Wesley, "Arise, My Soul, Arise," *A Collection of Hymns for the Use of the People Called Methodists* (London: John Mason, 1831), no. 202.
3. William Dumbrell, *The Search for Order: Biblical Eschatology in Focus* (Grand Rapids: Baker, 1994), 121.
4 In this day of broken families and abusive relationships, we must be careful to clarify that God's intended purpose for the family is not always the reality of individual family relationships. Sometimes parents do indeed relinquish their rights to respect and honor because of their sins against their children. God is the model for every human parent, rather than the other way around.
5. Karol Wojtyla, *Reflections on* Humanae Vitae (Boston: St. Paul Editions, 1986), 13–18.
6. A. N. Williams, "Instrument of the Union of Hearts: The Theology of Person-hood and the Bishop," *International Journal of Systematic Theology* 4, no. 3 (November 2002): 283.

CHAPTER 3: PERSONHOOD AND THE CONCEPT OF GOD

1. William Ury. *Trinitarian Personhood* (Eugene, Ore.: Wipf & Stock, 2001). Ury's work gives us an excellent study of the major figures in the development of Trinitarian thought with a very valuable treatment of Richard of St. Victor. This present work has found inspiration there.
2. Quoted in Erich Fromm, *Man for Himself* (London: Routledge & Kegan Paul, 1949), 35.
3. See Jaroslaw Kupczak, *Destined for Liberty* (Washington, D.C.: The Catholic University of America Press, 2000), 114.
4. Thomas Torrance, *The Christian Doctrine of God: One Being Three Persons* (Edinburgh: T. & T. Clark, 1996), 102.
5. Ibid., 170.
6. Gabriel Marcel, *The Mystery of Being: Faith and Reality*, vol. 2 (New York: Lanham, 1951), 8.
7. G. B. Caird, *The Language and Imagery of the Bible* (Grand Rapids: Eerdmans, 1997), 18.
8. Karl Barth, *Church Dogmatics*, 2.1 (Edinburgh: T. & T. Clark, 1957), 257–58.

9. Torrance, *Christian Doctrine of God,* 40.
10. For a perceptive discussion of Otto, see John Maquarrie's *In Search of Humanity* (New York: Crossroad, 1983), 202, 206.
11 John Zizioulas, *Being as Communion* (Crestwood, N.Y.: St. Vladimir's Seminary Press, 1985), 91, 269.
12. Robert Jenson, *Systematic Theology,* vol. 2 (New York: Oxford University Press, 1999), 63–68.
13. E. L. Mascall, *The Openness of Being* (Philadelphia: Westminster, 1971), 278.
14. Blaise Pascal, *Penseés,* trans. A. J. Krailsheimer (New York: Penguin, 1966), 347.
15. Stanley J. Grenz, *The Social God and the Relational Self: A Trinitarian Theology of the* Imago Dei (Louisville: Westminster John Knox, 2001), 96.
16. See also Philippians 2:3 and Romans 15:1–4.
17. Torrance, *Christian Doctrine of* God, 123.
18. See Martin Buber, *I and Thou* (New York: Scribner, 1957).
19. Karol Wojtyla, *The Jeweler's Shop* (San Francisco: St. Ignatius Press, 1982), 47–48.

CHAPTER 4: THE HUMAN PROBLEM

1. Emil Brunner, *Man in Revolt* (Philadelphia: Westminster, 1947), 136–37.
2. Ibid., 130.
3. Ibid., 480.
4. Gabriel Marcel, *The Mystery of Being: Reflection and Reality,* vol. 2 (New York: Lanham, 1951), 33–34.
5. Joe Sachs, "God of Abraham, Isaac, and Jacob," *The Great Ideas Today,* ed. Mortimer Adler (Chicago: Encyclopedia Britannica, 1988), 227.
6. Ibid.
7. See Lesslie Newbigin, *The Light Has Come* (Grand Rapids: Eerdmans, 1982), 39–40.
8. Robert Jenson, *America's Theologian: A Recommendation of Jonathan Edwards* (New York: Oxford University Press, 1988), 140, 148.
9. Ibid.
10. Friedrich Buchsel, *"eritheia,"* *Theological Dictionary of the New Testament,* ed. Gerhard Kittel, trans. Geoffrey W. Bromiley, vol. 2. (Grand Rapids: Eerdmans, 1964), 660.

CHAPTER 6: FULFILLMENT OF SALVATION: PERFECT LOVE

1. Edwin Hatch, "Breathe on Me, Breath of God," *The United Methodist Hymnal* (Nashville: United Methodist Publishing House, 1989), no. 420.
2. George Matheson, "Make Me a Captive, Lord," *The United Methodist Hymnal* (Nashville: United Methodist Publishing House, 1989), no. 421.
3. John Wesley, *A Plain Account of Christian Perfection* (London: Epworth, 1952), 90.

AUTHOR INDEX

SCRIPTURE INDEX

We want to hear from you. Please send your comments about this book to us in care of zreview@zondervan.com. Thank you.

ZONDERVAN™

GRAND RAPIDS, MICHIGAN 49530 USA

WWW.ZONDERVAN.COM